Jellema believes that colleges *can* put their operations on stable financial footing. By sharply defining their unique identities and promoting the special character of liberal, religious, or professional education which they alone offer, they can avoid direct competition with less costly public schools and retain their constituencies. In this way, private colleges can continue to contribute their important qualities of diversity, academic excellence, and intellectual freedom.

Based on a two-year survey conducted under the auspices of the Association of American Colleges, this book presents complete documentation of the fiscal health of 554 (75 percent) of our private four-year schools. The comprehensive data have been gathered from a truly representative sample of private higher education. No other contemporary study is so soundly based. Jellema's insights into fiscal operations and his specific findings and recommendations will be valuable to presidents, trustees, financial and admissions officers, planners, and faculty members in all private postsecondary institutions.

THE AUTHOR

WILLIAM W. JELLEMA is executive associate and research director of the Association of American Colleges.

From Red to Black?

*The Financial Status
of Private Colleges
and Universities*

William W. Jellema

From Red
to Black?

Jossey-Bass Publishers
San Francisco · Washington · London · 1973

FROM RED TO BLACK?
The Financial Status of Private Colleges and Universities
by William W. Jellema

Copyright © 1973 by: Jossey-Bass, Inc., Publishers
615 Montgomery Street
San Francisco, California 94111

&

Jossey-Bass Limited
3 Henrietta Street
London WC2E 8LU

Library of Congress Catalogue Card Number LC 73-7155

International Standard Book Number ISBN 0-87589-188-8

Manufactured in the United States of America

JACKET DESIGN BY WILLI BAUM

FIRST EDITION

Code 7330

The Jossey-Bass
Series in Higher Education

Preface

$\mathbb{F}$*rom Red to Black?*, which reports a study of the financial condition of private colleges and universities, documents what perceptive viewers of the higher education scene have feared: much of private higher education has been undergoing a financial crisis of grave proportions. Some institutions are still riding above it; most will ride through it—if it does not last too long; still others have succumbed or will succumb to it.

Many of the pressures which have brought about the financial condition of private colleges are also active in the affairs of tax-supported institutions. Therefore, the broad concern implicit here is for all higher education. Private institutions, however, have additional and special problems—of income, of student aid, of enrollment—that do not bite tax-supported institutions with the same force. The fiscal problems of private institutions are more acute, and their consequences more stark and immediate.

This book is based on data collected by the Association of American Colleges during the summers of 1970 and 1971 and on campus visits and local data obtained since that time. Nearly three-quarters of the accredited four-year private institutions supplied the data which form the basis for the analyses. The distribution of respondents in the analytical categories of this study is proportionate to the distribution in the total population of private institutions. Nonrespondents do not appear to be different from respondents. I be-

lieve, therefore, that the comprehensive data reported here have
been gathered from a representative sample of private higher education and provide a stable basis for reliable estimates of comparable
values for the total population. No other contemporary study is so
soundly based. (See Appendix for further description of the data
base.)

This study is important, however, only to the extent that
private higher education is important. If diversity and pluralism in
higher education are merely words, devoid of real meaning, then
these data may be equally devoid of significance. If, however, the
private sector is performing a function in our society that we cannot
afford to lose, then this study, which points to the possible loss of
that function, is important. If the attenuation of personal, academic,
and constitutional freedoms is at stake when the institutions that
lend expression to those freedoms are threatened, then this study,
which points to the reality of that threat, is important.

If private institutions are to continue, those who make
policy about higher education must confront the dual pricing system. We now have a system in which one sector is almost totally
underwritten by the tax dollar and another sector is largely dependent upon private support. It was not planned that way. Private
colleges, like a lot of other private institutions, came into being to
serve the public interest. Tax-supported institutions came into being
to serve other and overlapping aspects of that same public interest.

For a long time the dual pricing system had little apparent
consequence. The dollar difference was not great, and in most instances the perceived qualitative difference adequately compensated
for the price difference. Both these conditions have changed. According to Wynn's data[1] choosing a private rather than a public
higher education was, in 1964, a $650 (annual) decision. By 1971
it was a $1250 decision, and by 1976 it will be a $2000 decision.
While the difference in prices is increasing, the difference in quality
may be decreasing since many tax-supported institutions have significantly improved the quality of education offered in recent years.
In planning for the future, these differences must be taken into account, not ignored.

[1] G. Richard Wynn, "Liberal Arts College Pricing: Has the Market
Taken Over?" *Liberal Education*, 1972, *58*(3), 427.

The increasing price difference is a consequence of rapidly rising tuition in private higher education. This brings a further problem. As tuition increases, so must direct student aid; and since tuition is a major source of student aid funds, as student aid increases, so must tuition. This spiral is an outstanding reason for the deficit in the current accounts of many private institutions. At many of these colleges and universities, the difference between income and expenditures in the student aid account is precisely the deficit in the operating budget.

The student aid deficit is, in considerable measure, a consequence of the response of private higher education to the needs of the disadvantaged. At the same time, many private institutions are not able to respond to the financial needs of the middle class, which has been their major constituency. The trend suggests that only the very rich or the very poor may be able to attend a private college or university.

While severe financial stress has fallen on all institutions—large and small, simple and complex, northern and southern—it has severely hit very small undergraduate institutions in the Midwest. Very small institutions—especially those enrolling fewer than five hundred students—have a relatively high fixed cost per student and, unless they have endowment for a buffer, are more vulnerable to adverse trends in enrollment than are larger institutions. A drop in enrollment means that the cost per remaining student rises more precipitously than it does in larger institutions. This fixed cost includes a basic plant, a basic administrative structure, and especially a basic academic program whose proportions cannot be scaled down indefinitely. You can cut in half a recipe that calls for two eggs, but how do you cut it in half again? To be an institution of higher learning, an institution must offer a minimum of basic educational services.

The financial crunch has been felt in large, complex institutions because of conditions they share with smaller and less complex institutions—inflation, decline in the rate of income increase, rapid expansion of plant, deceleration of enrollment, expansion of student services, increases in security costs—and also because of their considerable involvement in research and their extensive expansion of program offerings to match the explosion of knowledge. Both research and program expansion require the commitment of institutional funds beyond those available from outside sources. And, if outside support declines, an added burden is laid upon institutional funds.

If private colleges and universities continue to run deficits of the magnitude they have been running in current accounts, many deficits will soon equal or exceed the total liquid assets of the institutions. (One quarter of the private colleges and universities are already dipping into their endowments.) The loss of liquid assets means the loss of flexibility and financial credibility; and the probability of further borrowing, additional debt service, and more retrenchment is increased. An institution however, can make only so much educational retrenchment without losing its identity in the academic world. Much of it, moreover, is one-shot retrenchment. After you do not wash the windows once, William Bowen has asked, what do you do for an encore? How do you not wash them again?

If expenditures continue to rise faster than income, the prospects are not pleasant to contemplate. Most private institutions of higher education can be maintained as viable structures however if the public can be made to recognize their value and provide the support these institutions must have. Support must be gathered throughout the nation in federal and state legislatures, in corporations and foundations, and among other constituencies. This is no time for complacency; but neither is it time for utter despair. What these pages reveal is the vision of the Ghost of Christmas Future—the situation that will exist if the course of institutional life is not changed.

An author's list of acknowledgments sometimes appears to be a meaningless necessity. Nothing could be further from the truth in this case. Seldom has one man been so indebted to so many. Friendship, professional collegiality, and concern for the fiscal fortunes of private higher education succeeded in eliciting a most generous outpouring of talent.

Elmer Jagow, Francis Finn, Peggy Heim, and Hans Jenny were present at the laying of the keel and at the launching. They did their best to see to it that the final product would float—and right side up. If it proves seaworthy, they deserve major credit.

Richard Wynn undertook the difficult job of editing the

data. In a relatively short period of time he, with an assistant or two, achieved by dint of hard work, insight, and persuasion what the Office of Education takes immeasurably longer to do with no greater return in accuracy. Highly tuned sensitivity to possible inaccuracies in reporting marked his invaluable performance.

Richard Panko and Ralph Broadstreet were lured into the project on the promise of a few hours graduate credit. They must have felt as though they had applied for an ordinary route and were assigned the task of providing regular mail delivery to the moon. The hundreds of volunteer hours contributed by these two young men in the wee hours of the morning became the hallmark of the project. Long after a military assignment took Ralph out of the area, Dick continued to produce the orderly data which was the lifeblood of this study even after he too was moved elsewhere. His delightful personality made "busted" programs and midnight telephone calls events that could always be tolerated and often enjoyed.

Congresswoman Edith Green was so convinced of the importance of this study that she placed the authority of her conviction behind my request to have Richard Panko released to this project from the United States Navy for a six week period—and succeeded. She added the making of naval history to her many other accomplishments that year.

American University provided most of the computer services, a contribution that was worth several thousand dollars to this project. Private higher education owes this one private institution a great debt of gratitude. It was not merely the generosity of its president, George Williams, that made this possible. Some other contributors were my friend Herbert Stutts, who, with Herbert Striner, ran initial interference, and Paul Howerton, who quickly sensed the importance of the study and put his powerful support behind it. He was joined by John Bassler. An extra effort also came from Robert Ogilvie, Richard Wingate, John Riddick, and others at the computer center.

Richard Sullivan was responsible for the initial grant for this project from the Carnegie Corporation. Moreover his interest extended beyond to provide moral as well as financial support; he read the entire manuscript and offered helpful suggestions. Howard Barr and James Hosey of the United States Steel Foundation brought needed additional financial support to the project. The General Electric Corporation was also financially supportive.

Sharvy Umbeck, William Johnson, Robert Meyer, and colleagues Eric Wormald and John Gillis made enormously helpful suggestions at the outset and on the special preliminary report. Eric's wise counsel was especially evident in the days just before that report was published.

Robert Hartman, Blair Stewart, Kurt Hertzfeld, Earl Cheit, Theodore Drews, and Howard Bowen all read the penultimate draft of the manuscript and made me the beneficiary of their wisdom. They are not to be blamed if I did not successfully follow their sound advice.

Laurie Fifield Tongren, Marti Patchell, Rita Leiphart, Judith Mattson, Michael Green, John Creager, Ralph Smith, and Brook Hedge all assisted with various aspects of the work, and Linda Ball, my secretary, with easy grace and competence, assembled the final manuscript, persuading unruly pages to follow one another in order.

Last best. My wife, Lois, typed, prepared graphics, offered editorial oversight, read proof, and worked with raw data when we were too short of time or money to use the computer. She was regularly abandoned nights and weekends and shared our camping trailer with several hundredweight of computer printout. Through it all she did not lose her sense of humor and successfully pretended that I was not at times perilously close to losing mine. I am most grateful to her.

There are others whose names I do not know. These are persons who were called upon by one of the persons named above or who were ready at the other end of a telephone when I needed them. To them, too, my thanks.

This book is for Bill, for Cal, and for Jon.

September 1973   WILLIAM W. JELLEMA
Washington, D.C.

Contents

From Red to Black?

The Financial Status of Private Colleges and Universities

"And like a lobster boiled, the morn
From black to red began to turn"
                    Samuel Butler

The heat's been on the college, too,
And lobster-like its ink changed hue

Now when the lobster cools, its shell
Retains the shade it wears so well

But college hopes its ink turns back
From red on red to basic black
                    W. W. J.

Financial Past, Present, and Future

❀❀❀❀❀❀❀❀❀❀❀❀❀❀

Intimations of the depressing financial picture of private higher education did not first appear in 1968. Hints of a growing crisis could be found earlier in steadily rising costs, a widening tuition gap between public and private higher education, mounting inflation, an expansion of student services and academic programs, and a declining rate of enrollment. The fiscal year 1968 became a "base year," however, because it was the starting point for the income and expenditure data collected for this financial study of private higher education. So it may be useful to say something about the fiscal situation in private institutions as perceived in 1968.

Base Year: 1968

We were told, in a report of Committee Z of the AAUP for 1967–68, that faculty compensation had risen an average of

$4357 since 1960–61. Further evidence supplied by William Baumol of Princeton noted that expenditure per student in private institutions increased 65 percent more rapidly than prices in the economy as a whole during the decade which ended with fiscal 1968. Moreover, for the benefit of those who think that the cause of this increase can be laid at the door of research, Baumol wrote that, even exclusive of research, the cost per student had risen 50 percent more rapidly.

If the trend continued uncorrected, he prophesied, the cost per student in current dollars would rise in forty years to sixteen times the 1968 level, and total expenditures (not per student) in constant dollars would rise in forty years to more than sixty-five times the 1968 level.[1]

A study conducted in Texas[2] indicated that, if the trend from 1963–64 to 1967–68 was to continue, by 1985 the cost per student (in constant 1968 dollars) in major independent universities in Texas would be $36,859 and the cost per student in senior (four-year) colleges in the state would be $17,074. If the percentage covered by tuition were the same in 1985 as in 1968, the student at a private university would be asked to pay $17,324 per year and the student at a senior college would be confronted with a tuition charge of $9695.

A study of ten prestigious colleges and universities published in 1967 showed a progressive decline in the use of black ink between 1961–66 with the need for more red ink than black by 1967.[3]

In 1968 a friend sent me an excerpt from the annual report of a college president that read: "During all the years of its development as a church-related university, [this institution] has experienced a great frequency of financial crises. Only the Almighty's repeated answering of the sustained prayers raised by the school's

[1] William J. Baumol and Peggy Heim, "On the Financial Prospects for Higher Education: The Annual Report on the Economic Status of the Profession, 1967–68," *AAUP Bulletin*, 1968, *54*(2), 184, 188.

[2] Liaison Committee on Texas Private Colleges and Universities, "Pluralism and Partnership: The Case for the Dual System of Higher Education," n.d., p. 41.

[3] *Study of Rising Costs at Ten Universities* (Ithaca, N.Y.: Cornell University, 1957), cited by Earl F. Cheit, *The New Depression in Higher Education* (New York: McGraw-Hill, 1971).

courageous board and administration has prevented many potential catastrophes from occurring." Then, with unconscious irony which emphasizes the fact that the financial crisis visible at least by 1968 was no common one, the president's report continued: "Now, however, the seriousness of the commitments necessary to implement the university's ambitious program requires that the needed degree and continuity of support be more clearly defined and more definitely assured." "Obviously," my informant commented, "things are in one hell of a mess!"

This, then, was the way the situation looked in 1968, the base year, and by far the best financial year in this study in terms of operating balance. From that point, an already bad situation deteriorated rapidly. As Pogo might have said looking at the following three years of financial data, "From here on down, it's all uphill."

Spread of Deficit Operating Budgets

In the years since, costs have continued to rise: instruction costs are higher with no increase in productivity; building costs are higher; maintenance costs are higher; security costs are higher; many students and their parents are demanding wall-to-wall services; while inflation has continued to blur any kind of financial datum line. Corporate giving is down, and enrollment growth has been halted.

Looking at net surplus or deficit for the current operating fund in 1968, we find that the "average" (or mean) institution (a gross but useful trend indicator) finished its fiscal year with a deficit. The data indicated that this deficit would quintuple one year later, the fiscal year ending (for most institutions) June 30, 1970. This prediction, as we shall see, was optimistic.

Looking at the average institution in each of nine geographical regions, however, we see a somewhat different picture emerging. The break between 1968 and 1969 does not appear so sharp. In some regions the average institution was already running a deficit in 1968; in other regions the decline into deficits was delayed until 1970. Specifically, in six regions the average institution was showing a surplus when it ended its fiscal year in June 1968. In three regions, geographically separated from one another, the average institution ended that year with a deficit. One year later, the average institution in three more regions finished the year with a deficit. By June 1970, membership in the deficit club was complete, with the average institution in every region firmly in the red. These data for 540 private colleges and universities are presented in Table 1. The data for 1969–70 and 1970–71 are based upon institutional projections.

Table 1. NET CURRENT FUND SURPLUS OR DEFICIT FOR THE
AVERAGE INSTITUTION: BY GEOGRAPHICAL REGIONS
(in thousands): 1968–1971

Region	1967–68	1968–69	1969–70	1970–71
All Institutions	39	−20	−103	−115
Pacific	4	13	−52	−46
Mountain	6	−13	−50	−116
West South Central	−81	−97	−149	−62
East South Central	14	−46	−87	−37
West North Central	54	0	−116	−76
East North Central	−23	−56	−147	−143
South Atlantic	126	50	−47	−87
Mid-Atlantic	108	14	−92	−189
New England	−19	−137	−141	−151

If we take a different vantage point to examine the trend, a similar picture emerges. Statistically summarized and arranged in five degree level categories (see Appendix), the financial condition of all private colleges and universities is seen to have steadily worsened. By 1968–69, private institutions in every degree category but one, taken as a statistical average, were showing a deficit. Not a contrived deficit, not an indirect student aid deficit (which all private institutions have been running for years), not the deficit administrators sometimes submit to their boards to stimulate giving, not the deficit sometimes reported before annual gift money or contributed services provided by a religious order are included as income, but an actual current fund deficit: akin to the kind you and I have when our total actual expenditures are larger than our total actual income.

Some individual institutions in each of these categories were running deficits in 1967–68 and even earlier; others continued to run surpluses in 1968–69; but the average institution in each of the five categories finished in the black in 1967–68 and, in every category but one, finished in the red in 1968–69, one year later. So much for the good news.

The Projection Game

One end of our four years of data is fixed to the year 1968. The other is pinned to 1971, a year whose fiscal fortune was not yet fact when the data were collected. These projected data are, perforce, spongy and uneven. Even the data for the fiscal year 1969–70 gathered in our first questionnaire were, for most of the institutions in our study, a projection. They do not have the same kind of reliability as data for the first two years.

The making of projections is a spooky enterprise. A summation of predictions made at the local level appeared to have, however, a certain earthy reliability. Such predictions are affected by word from the admissions office; worries from the development office; intimations of still higher costs; speculation about the amount of tuition increase the local constituency will bear; rumors of the establishment or further development of a local junior college; grim decisions of where to cut back, in what order and when—all compounded by hopes and fears concerning the national economy. What you may lose in lack of sophisticated understanding of how national movements will affect the future of private higher education may be more than compensated for by the intimate awareness of local factors. Small miscalculations, however, can have consequences of considerable magnitude. If, in a relatively modest budget of five million dollars, either income or expenditures prove to be off by as little as 1 or 2 percent, the result will be a disparity of fifty thousand to one hundred thousand dollars. Since both income and expenditures are categories of many items, this much fluctuation can take place quite easily.

Some institutions overestimated the deficit they would incur in 1969–70 (fiscal 1970). Others, a larger number, underestimated. For 1971 an even larger number underestimated the deficits they would incur. Hope, a little inebriated by unwarranted optimism, seems to outrun despair in projecting future income. For example, some institutions that showed a stable or even declining amount of gifts and grants for the three years beginning in 1968 suddenly projected an astonishing increase in unrestricted gifts. Perhaps they anticipated something the reviewer of questionnaires could not: perhaps a highly favorable will was expected to be probated in that year. But to one not privy to such inside information it looked more like a desperate fiction invented to project a balanced budget.

Similar unrestrained enthusiasm is sometimes seen in the projection of tuition and fees. The 1971 budget for some colleges, if not balanced, at least appeared less tinted with scarlet because of a sudden increase in income received from tuition and fees. Since it is both probable that tuition had already been steadily rising and unlikely that some sharp increase in tuition charges is what was being contemplated, it must have been that the college expected to have more students paying slightly higher tuition.

A check of the figures on enrollment confirms this expectation. An institution which had been experiencing a decline in applications and enrollment—sharp, graduated, or uneven—might project a sudden large increase in its freshman enrollment. For a given institution this is always possible—improbable, but possible. By dint of heroic effort, some institutions can turn norms, averages, and other statistics on their ear. But not nationally. Not enough students of the academic quality that these colleges and universities have traditionally admitted are available to make such optimistic projections come true. While individual institutions may with justice be exhorted to work hard on student recruitment, it is both unreasonable and irresponsible to look at the total national scene and say, "If those colleges would just get off their duffs and go looking for students, they could eliminate their deficits." This simply is not so.

Financial projection patterns, however, are by no means identical, as the following comparison of two groups of institutions indicates. Institutions that ran a relatively small deficit in 1969 (less than twenty-five thousand dollars)—of which there were approximately fifty in the nation as a whole—had, typically, run a surplus the year before and projected a deficit for 1970 nearly nine times as large as the deficit they ran in 1969. For 1971 they projected a deficit only two-thirds the size of the previous year. To call this an improvement in their financial condition is like calling a rise in temperature from ninety degrees below zero to sixty degrees below zero a warming trend. Yet, it is instructive to notice the basis for this relatively milder financial climate.

Almost all expenditure items were projected by these institutions to continue to rise in 1971 at about the same rate as earlier. The warming trend difference therefore must have been in income —but not in all income areas. These institutions projected declines in income for some items and hoped for no dramatic increases in any other areas save two: tuition income and gift and grant income. The latter was projected to jump 25 percent for 1971 even though income from this source had declined the previous year by nearly 6 percent.

As to tuition and fee income, the figures themselves are not quite so dramatic. Income from this source was projected to increase in 1971 over the previous year by 12 percent compared with increases of 11 percent and 12 percent in the prior two years. The nearly 40 percent (compounded) increase in tuition income in 1971 over 1968 is not as dramatic as the expectation of a continuing significant rise in tuition revenue despite the evidence for a declining pool of applicants. However, the institutions did not expect even these increases in income to redeem them from a deficit posture but merely to introduce a warming breeze into their Antarctica of deficits.

By comparison, the approximately fifty institutions in the nation that in 1969 ran a relatively large deficit—between one hundred thousand and one hundred fifty thousand dollars—projected a similar trend line (that is, a deficit the following year nearly eight times larger followed by a projected improvement in 1971 which cut the 1970 deficit by less than half) but for quite different reasons. They foresaw no improvement in any income source in 1971. The reason for the milder anticipated deficit lies, in this case, in reduced expenditures. In every current fund expenditure item, these institutions expected to spend less than they had the year before. Enough less, in fact, so that, even though they also projected a declining income, they expected to incur a lesser deficit.

This group appears to have been more realistic than those institutions with a smaller deficit that expected improvement by a

marked rise in income. Perhaps a larger deficit has a more sobering
effect on future planning.

If so, there were plenty of sober institutions. Collectively,
higher education carries an indebtedness on its physical plant of over
three billion dollars and a current fund indebtedness (in 1969) of
nearly half a billion dollars on a current fund budget of about five
billion dollars. The total deficit reported by the institutions in our
study for 1968 and 1969 was 93 million dollars. They expected
to run additional deficits in the next two years that would total 173
million dollars. This expectation, as we shall see, proved optimistic;
but even these 266 million dollars, by extrapolation to all of private
higher education, would amount to nearly 370 million dollars.

Spread of Deficits

The mind that no longer boggles at billions is sure not to be
alarmed at 370 millions. The staggering sums spent on space ex-
ploration or on overruns in the development of military weapons do
make this rather a small amount. The amount of federal aid for
which major businesses in their deficit situations have petitioned
makes the college deficit look like small potatoes. The federal budget
for fiscal 1973 runs to 2217 pages—an average of 111 million dollars in expenditures per page. The deficit in private colleges is equal
to only 3.3 pages. Even private higher education, if it were a collective whole, would not find 370 million dollars a staggering amount.
The reason is that other institutions were running offsetting surpluses sufficiently large so that the net current fund deficit for 1969
was only 0.3 percent of the combined total current fund expenditure
budgets of all private institutions of higher learning. Their projected
net deficit for 1970 was only 1.4 percent of that year's current fund
budget. (It turned out to be 1.8 percent, but even this is not an hor-
rendous figure—for a collective entity.)

But private higher education is not a collective whole. It is
many institutions situated in many different sections of the country,
large and small, church-related and independent, baccalaureate
degree granting and doctoral degree granting, some emphasizing
teaching and others massively engaged in research. Individual institutions present a wider variety of surplus and deficit patterns than

tables and graphs of gross statistics can reveal. Some marched steadily from a surplus or small deficit in 1968 into deeper and deeper deficits. Others were doing well and continued to do so; while still others moved helter skelter over the four years from surplus to deficit, back to surplus and back to deficit, or vice versa. Indeed, at least one example of virtually any surplus-deficit pattern possible may be found.

In every enrollment group, for example, at least a quarter of the institutions in each of the four years was running a surplus. (Indeed, when we solicited these earlier data, one-fourth of the institutions reported or anticipated no net deficit in any of the four years.) Also, as Table 2 makes clear, one-quarter of the institutions in every enrollment range ran a deficit in each of the four years. In only one of the enrollment ranges—the Large (2001–4000)—did the median institution expect to stay in the black. (The figures for all private institutions combined are, coincidentally, the same as those for the medium enrollment group.) In reading Table 2, note that in the Largest group, for instance, the designation "D 6" for the lower quartile means that one-quarter of the institutions in that group was running deficits of three hundred thousand to six hundred thousand dollars or more during 1967–68 and 1968–69. By 1970–71, one-quarter in this group was projecting deficits of 2.5 million dollars or more.

Not only was the number of institutions reporting deficits increasing, but the extent of the deficits they were running was increasing. In 1968, 35 percent of the private institutions reported deficits; in 1969, 43 percent. Next the figure jumped to 58 percent and then increased an additional 2 percent the following year. The increase in the size of the collective net deficit after 1970 is due more to the extent of the deficits in institutions with deficits than to increasing numbers of institutions with deficits.

A relatively high percentage of the large, complex private universities began to run deficits early. In 1969, 43 percent of all private colleges and universities ran deficits. (An additional 20 percent had budgets that either broke even or ran a surplus less than twenty-five thousand dollars.) However, 47 percent of all private Limited Doctor's institutions (institutions offering the doctorate in three areas or less) and 54 percent of the Doctor's institutions (institutions offering the doctorate in four areas or more) ran a deficit.

Table 2. CURRENT FUND SURPLUS OR DEFICIT RANGES, SHOWING
MEDIAN AND QUARTILE: BY ENROLLMENT GROUPS: 1968–1971

	1967–68	1968–69	1969–70	1970–71
	(actual data)		(projected data)	
Smallest (500 or less)				
upper quartile	S 2	S 3	S 1	S 1
median	0	S 1	D 1	D 1
lower quartile	D 2	D 3	D 3	D 3
Small (501–1000)				
upper quartile	S 3	S 2	S 1	S 1
median	S 2	S 1	D 1	D 1
lower quartile	D 2	D 3	D 4	D 4
Medium (1001–2000)				
upper quartile	S 3	S 1	S 1	S 1
median	S 1	S 3	D 1	0
lower quartile	D 2	D 3	D 4	D 4
Large (2001–4000)				
upper quartile	S 5	S 5	S 3	S 3
median	S 2	S 1	0	0
lower quartile	D 1	D 4	D 4	D 5
Largest (over 4000)				
upper quartile	S 6	S 6	S 4	S 1
median	S 2	S 1	D 4	D 4
lower quartile	D 6	D 6	D 7	D 8

Key

S (surplus) or D (deficit)
0 zero balance
1 less than $25,000
2 between $25,000 and $50,000
3 between $50,000 and $100,000
4 between $100,000 and $150,000
5 between $150,000 and $300,000
6 between $300,000 and $600,000
7 over $600,000
8 over $2,500,000

Bachelor's, Limited Master's, and Master's institutions were, at 41, 43, and 43 percent, at or near the norm for all private institutions combined.

As judged by this combined percentage, the Pacific, Mountain, West South Central, and West North Central regions were disproportionately represented by institutions running deficits in 1969, as can be seen from the following percentage figures:

Pacific	66
Mountain	71
West South Central	57
East South Central	42
West North Central	51
East North Central	40
South Atlantic	33
Mid Atlantic	36
New England	40

Although the median institution in each enrollment group in 1969 was running a small surplus, the percentage actually running a deficit varied from one group to the other. In ascending order of enrollment size, these percentages were: Smallest—38, Small—44, Medium—46, Large—39, Largest—43.

Roman Catholic-related institutions at 44 percent and those independent of church relationship at 42 percent, struck the 1969 deficit norm of 43 percent almost exactly. High in relation to this norm were institutions related to the American Lutheran Church (56 percent), Lutheran Church in America (53 percent), American Baptist Convention, United Presbyterian Church U.S.A., United Church of Christ, and Disciples of Christ (all at 50 percent). Low were institutions related to the Southern Baptist Church (24 percent), Mennonite (29 percent), and Church of the Brethren (zero percent!).

One-quarter of these private institutions were running deficits of less than 2 percent of their current fund expenditure budgets even in projected 1970–71. The median deficit institution, however, ran for the four years a deficit that was, progressively, 2.7, 3.2, 3.8, and 4.2 percent of current fund expenditures. The quarter of institutions in the worst degree of deficit ran deficits that began, in successive years, at 5.8, 6.6, 7.6, and 7.4 percent of their current fund budgets and ran as high as 29.1 percent.

Smaller institutions were particularly vulnerable. Nineteen percent of the Smallest institutions were running deficits that were 8 percent or more of their current fund expenditure budgets; 16 percent of the Small institutions were running deficits of this magnitude; 8 percent of the Medium institutions were suffering as severely as this; while only 2 percent of the Large and 5 percent of the Largest were having deficits in this range.

Individual institutions, no matter how perilous their situation as judged by the statistical company they keep or by the implications of their data, may, like Pauline, be saved from imminent disaster by the fortuitous appearance and heroic action of some savior —a magnificent gift, a substantial increase in enrollment, the favorable effects of legislation—or by native intelligence which enables them to outwit the financial villain and escape. But statistics take note of the opposite possibilities as well: the disaffected donor, declining enrollment, the absence or ineffectual results of state legislation.

Private colleges and universities were apprehensive at this point in the study (summer 1970), and they had reason to be. Most colleges in the red were staying in the red and getting redder, while colleges in the black were generally growing grayer. Taken collectively, their days as viable institutions, capable of serving the public with quality and strength, appeared to be numbered.

Follow-up Data

That the projections—grim though they were—were often based upon unwarranted optimism was confirmed in a follow-up survey made to determine what the actual figures had been for 1970, what the respondents' updated projection was for fiscal year 1971 (which was just closing), and, in general, how they viewed their financial prospects for the next two years.

A popcorn pattern was evident, according to which individual institutions jump into the black only to fall again into the red, while other institutions are doing the reverse. Some institutions were doing better than they had expected—although that often meant less of a deficit, not a surplus—while other institutions were doing worse than their projections. The split appeared to be about even in numbers of institutions, with the numerical edge going to those doing worse than expected—and, if worse, then much worse.

This follow-up study was focused on the 507 colleges and universities that were included in the earlier report. When those who reported doing better were aggregated with those who reported doing worse, the experience proved gravely worse than expected. Together they had projected a deficit of $104,000 per institution. It was depressing, therefore, to discover that the actual deficit for the average institution among these 507 was $131,000—$27,000 (or 26 percent) worse than anticipated.

The gloom deepened in learning that their financial future was more grim than their earlier data indicated: their projections for 1971 were more dismal than they had been a year earlier. These 507 institutions had projected a deficit of $120,000 per institution, which they now expected to go to $158,000—nearly eight times the deficit incurred by the average institution only two years earlier.

The picture is no more heartening when examined region by region (see Table 3). In every region but two, 1971 was predicted to be a year of greater deficits than 1970 proved to be. In one of these regions 1971 was foreseen as likely to be only slightly less bad than 1970. Only in the Mountain region—a mere eight institutions reporting—was 1971 expected to prove better than 1970. Especially distressing is that in four of the regions—West South Central, East South Central, West North Central, and East North Central—the average institution that had looked forward to an improved position now predicted that it would have slipped into deeper deficits when the books closed on 1971. In short, in every region but one (the Mountain region) the average institution predicted a deficit more severe for 1971 than it had foreseen a year earlier.

All of these figures swim submerged in a sea of red ink. No longer—as in the data for 1968 and even 1969—do we have the average institution in any region in the black or even on the break-even surface. It would take Pollyanna to derive much comfort from the fact that 1971 was projected to be slightly "better" in one small region than 1970 proved to be. Even in that region one can drown as quickly in 43 fathoms of red ink as in 116.

Table 3. FORECAST AND ACTUAL DEFICITS FOR AVERAGE INSTITUTION (in thousands): 1970–1971

	1970			1971 Projection		
	Projected Figure	Actual Figure	Difference	Original Figure	Updated Projection	Difference
Geographic Regions						
All Institutions Combined (507 Institutions)	−104	−131	−27	−120	−158	−38
Pacific	−45	−52	−7	−52	−76	−24
Mountain	−50	−85	−35	−116	−43	+73
West South Central	−160	−181	−21	−71	−250	−179
East South Central	−75	−67	+8	−31	−84	−53
West North Central	−116	−112	+4	−74	−135	−61
East North Central	−163	−164	−1	−157	−162	−5
South Atlantic	−48	−120	−72	−95	−144	−49
Mid-Atlantic	−82	−144	−62	−177	−183	−6
New England	−158	−191	−33	−186	−279	−93
Degree Levels						
Bachelor's	−52	−54	−2	−52	−64	−12
Limited Master's	−74	−70	+4	−69	−81	−12
Master's	−135	−112	+23	−186	−129	+57
Limited Doctor's	+36	−271	−307	−48	−229	−181
Doctor's	−643	−883	−240	−770	−1138	−368
Enrollment Groups						
Smallest	−44	−34	+10	−66	−58	+8
Small	−71	−75	−4	−77	−86	−9
Medium	−75	−69	+6	−57	−83	−31
Large	−28	−51	−23	−61	−33	+28
Largest	−405	−636	−231	−544	−789	−245

Figure 1 charts projected data and actual data for institutions in each of nine geographical regions, with a national summary for general comparison. The dotted lines show projections. The line begins at the point of the projected deficit for fiscal 1970 for the average institution in that area and culminates at the point of the projected deficit for fiscal 1971. Note that we no longer need to talk of surpluses as well as deficits. All points on the figure are deficits in thousands of dollars.

The solid line shows the updated fiscal data gathered one year later. Its beginning point is the actual net current fund deficit for the average institution in each region for fiscal 1970. The line ends at the updated projection for 1971. Remember that the one region which appears to show a much improved outlook for 1971, the Mountain region, embraces but eight institutions of the 507 reporting. Not all regions are equal. Some, as George Orwell would say, are more equal than others.

Note that even this picture masks a grimmer reality. Behind these deficits lie curtailed operations, abbreviated departments, underdeveloped academic programs, languishing aspirations, and curbed creativity. The deficits are this great even though such cutbacks have been made. If they had not been, the deficits would surely have been much higher.

When the anticipations are compared by degree groupings with actual 1970 and updated 1971 data (Table 3), we see that in two cases 1970 was fiscally better than had been foreseen and for one group—Master's institutions—the forecast for 1971 looked better than it did a year earlier; the betterment, in this case, being a smaller deficit than was previously expected.

The deficits for Ph.D. granting institutions are substantially larger than those of institutions offering only lower degrees. Although many smaller baccalaureate institutions are less able to bear their deficits than some large doctoral granting ones, an annual deficit of over one million dollars is a formidable figure for any institution even if substantially endowed and blessed with prosperous alumni. This, after all, is the figure after the annual earning from endowment and the annual giving from alumni have been entered. These are institutions with very substantial program commitments that cannot be curtailed swiftly or easily.

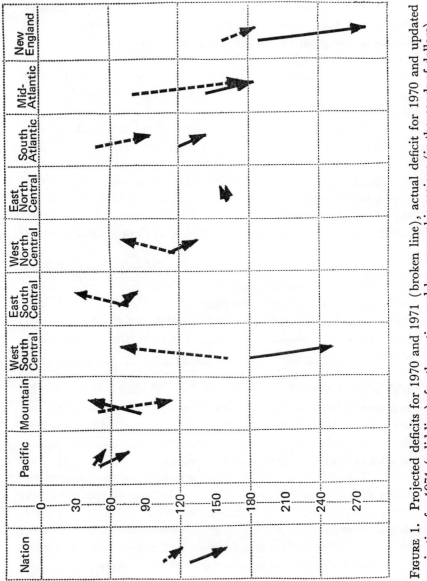

FIGURE 1. Projected deficits for 1970 and 1971 (broken line), actual deficit for 1970 and updated projection for 1971 (solid line), for the nation and by geographic regions (in thousands of dollars).

The baccalaureate and master's degree granting institutions show themselves, as a group, to be reasonably accurate in their projections. For 1970 the Bachelor's group hit its forecast almost on the nose and Limited Master's institutions were off by only 5 percent. Doctor's institutions proved to be off 37 percent in their collective forecast. They thought that they would suffer smaller deficits than proved to be the case. The even greater disparity between forecast and actuality for Limited Doctor's institutions was, however, compounded by a separate factor: during the intervening year the cold fingers of the deficit plague settled upon a small number in this group that had been "average raisers" the year before. Table 3 supplies figures for these degree groups.

The same analysis made by enrollment groups reveals that for three groups the actual deficit for 1970 was greater than they had expected, and that, also for three groups, the updated projection for 1971 was for a deficit more severe than they had expected a year earlier. Only the Smallest had favorable comparisons in both instances. The Small and, ominously, the Largest were disappointed both times.

Averages are helpful but they are plainly unable to reveal the range and diversity of the financial experience of specific institutions. Figure 2 attempts to be specific. It presents a comparison between the surpluses or deficits experienced in 1968 and the surpluses or deficits incurred in 1971. The 1971 data were solicited during the early summer of 1971. Since the books had not been formally closed for most institutions, the surpluses or deficits reported must be considered anticipated. If the experience of the previous year repeated itself, however, these data will be found in most cases to have understated the magnitude of the deficits. Each institution appears on the figure once and may be located both with reference to its surplus or deficit position in 1968 and with reference to its surplus or deficit position in 1971.

Institutions located in the sparsely populated lower right quadrant are those few that mastered the trick of exchanging a deficit in 1968 for a surplus in 1971. Institutions located in the upper right quadrant—not heavily populated either—had surpluses both years. With few exceptions, moreover, their surpluses were not large. However, the clustering around the center of the figure may mask

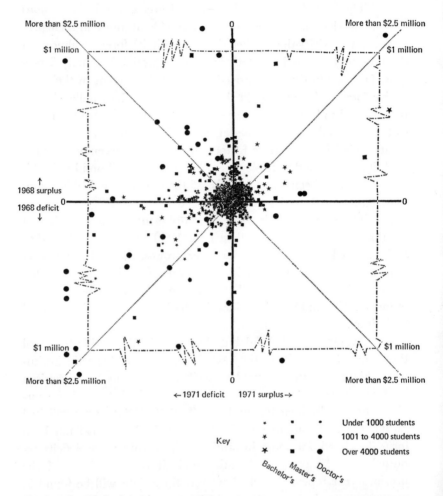

FIGURE 2.   Relation between 1968 and 1971 surpluses and deficits, all private institutions.

the magnitude of the deficits (and surpluses) that some institutions —especially smaller ones—were running. A deficit of only fifty thousand or one hundred thousand dollars can be a serious matter in a small institution.

The left side of the figure, where the population is densest, locates institutions running deficits in 1971. Those in the lower left quadrant reported deficits both years. Those in the upper left quadrant had surpluses in 1968 and deficits in 1971. (A symbol located above the dotted line in this quadrant indicates that the institution ran a surplus in 1968 that exceeded the magnitude of the deficit incurred in 1971. Those located below the dotted line had deficits in 1971 greater than the surpluses in 1968.) The "movement" of the figure (like political attitudes at Harvard) is to the left.

What is perhaps most striking about the lower left quadrant is the group of universities arrayed along the far left. All experienced deficits of varying magnitude in 1968 and were driven to the wall, so to speak, in 1971 with deficits of 2.5 million dollars—or more: four, six, eight million dollars. One large doctoral institution, it may be noted, ran deficits of 2.5 million dollars or more in both years.

Prospective Demise Based on 1968–1969 Deficits

One question that quickly captures the imagination of those who become interested in the financial problems of higher education is "How many colleges will fold and how soon?" The death of a college is a dramatic event, while an imbalance in its statement of accounts is not. Journalists go looking for pictures of a gothic Old Main with ivy creeping into the broken windows, the front door boarded up, and a discreet For Sale sign peeping over the tall weeds of what was once a well manicured lawn. They want to accompany this picture with a statement of numbers—how many and when? The question is much more complex than it appears on the surface. The wisest response is probably "impossible to tell." Another tempting response is a Delphic utterance based upon convoluted formulae that would make the Gordian knot look like a cub scout's "granny" by comparison.

The number of threads that must be wound into the formulae, involving local as well as national conditions and trends, is large indeed. But even if these calculations were perfectly made they would be unable to take into account the extent to which a college could continue to exist by altering its purposes and becoming a new kind of institution, by persuading donors to give and lenders to lend beyond normal expectations, by curtailing services, or by decreasing the quality of its program. The calculations would also imperfectly include a reckoning of the possible impact of favorable state legislation supporting private higher education, of changes in the tax laws encouraging philanthropy, of shifts in manpower needs or in student aspirations for higher education.

Moreover, an institution can fold in more than one way. It may cease to function in one place but move to another. It may cease to function as a private institution but continue as a publicly supported one. It may merge with another institution. It may declare formal bankruptcy. Or it may simply cease to be. Quietly, in the still of the night, as it were, it simply passes from the scene. In the past, such colleges usually have been small, seldom four-year, and even less frequently accredited. When they sink they leave only a faint ripple to mark their passing.

But this quiet scene may be violently upset in the near future. Only a little miscalculation could send a major institution to the bottom. If so, it will not be with a tiny ripple but with a tidal wave of attention and reaction.

Using the data at hand, I could only ask the limited question "How many private institutions have liquid assets to support another year like fiscal 1969?" Specifically, with no greater disparity between current fund revenue and current expenditure than existed in fiscal 1969 and assuming no change in the economy, in the operation of the institution, or in its fiscal imbalance, "How many years can how many private colleges and universities last before incurring deficits that equal or exceed their total liquid assets?"

Total liquid assets was defined as the combination of any unappropriated surplus funds, any other reserves—even though they may not be fully funded—and all funds functioning as endowment. We have no way of knowing, I repeat, how additionally persuasive a president and his board may be to prospective donors or possible lenders beyond the powers they have already demonstrated. Moreover, some colleges loosely call their funds functioning as endowment by the term *unrestricted endowment,* a term which has another meaning when used precisely. We have no way of determining accurately the amount of money covered by this semantic blanket that would be available as liquid assets; but it is probably small. We do not know how many institutions may have disposable assets other than liquid reserves—an urban university, say, with a residence hall to sell to a neighboring hospital or with other readily cashable fixed assets. Nor can we do more than speculate about the possible hypothecation of true endowment funds, a policy of desperation which we fear may become attractive to some institutions. Nor do we here reckon with an institution's ability and willingness to cut back on programs or operations in order to save money or with its ability to find and eliminate any "fat" in the institution. Some institutions can tighten the belt on the organizational slack. Others are already at the last notch.

Perhaps an additional comment or two about bankruptcy and cash flow are in order before presenting the arithmetic. Bankruptcy—the inability to discharge obligations to creditors—is approached when liabilities exceed assets, both liquid and other. A college, however, may not be able to realize its fixed assets. To give up its fixed assets, moreover, may be to give up the ghost. This can be true in the world of business, as well, but a business may have some additional assets to manipulate. It may, for instance, be able to reduce its inventory. Virtually the only assets a college can manipulate, however, are the funds we have summarized as liquid assets. For this reason, a college can reach the end of its rope before liabilities exceed total assets. It can be finished before it is bankrupt.

But colleges have one advantage over most businesses: they collect in advance. Most businesses get their money only after they have delivered goods and services; colleges and universities get their money before performing. Thus, they can cover current gaps between income and expenditure with the flow of cash. But this procedure masks the difficulty into which the college has slipped. Though an institution may stay afloat by using cash flow as a kind of life preserver, its buoyancy is not unlimited, and, in any event, this constitutes a borrowing against current funds.

It is not a simple case of being safe in the ark of liquid assets or drowned in the red ink of bankruptcy. The data assembled here look only at the current fund of the institution. Moreover, the year-end statement is a single frame in a moving picture of highs and lows in the financial position. The point in financial time we are seeking to identify here, however, is the moment when next year's oil is used to lubricate this year's operation.

Assuming business as usual, then, how many institutions can continue to run deficits the magnitude they ran in 1969 before reaching this point? Under standard accounting procedures, as distinct from cash flow management, the study found that 107 private accredited four-year colleges and universities could go less than one year if they continued to run deficits as large as those in 1969. Seventy-four of them could not last even a fraction of a year. They had exhausted their total liquid assets. Under a policy of business as usual, only the line of cash flow would keep them from going deeper into debt or out of business.

Twenty-one of these seventy-four institutions were in the West North Central region—Iowa, Kansas, Minnesota, Missouri, Nebraska, North and South Dakota. Another fourteen were in the East North Central region—Illinois, Indiana, Michigan, Ohio, and Wisconsin. Ten were in the Pacific region—California, Oregon, Washington, Hawaii, and Alaska: And nine were in the Mid-Atlantic region—New York, New Jersey, and Pennsylvania. Two-thirds (52) of them were baccalaureate institutions, and an additional thirteen were institutions offering the master's degree in three areas or less.

The enrollment group with the largest number of colleges near the end of their string was the Small group (see Table 2). Nearly half (thirty-five) the total (seventy-four) were in this size grouping. The next largest number (twenty-six) was in the Medium group. As a percentage, however, the group with the largest amount of institutions with no more liquid assets was the Smallest group. The seven institutions of this size with no more liquid assets were 21 percent of the total number of institutions of that size in the study. The thirty-five institutions in the Small group constituted 19 percent of their total.

Of all the Roman Catholic–related institutions in the study, twenty (13 percent) had exhausted their liquid assets. Also in this condition were twelve Methodist colleges (20 percent of their total), sixteen independents (10 percent of their total), eight institutions related with the United Presbyterians U.S.A. (24 percent of their total), and four of the sixteen institutions related to the Lutheran Church in America.

If their deficits continued at the same level as in 1969, 145 institutions (the above 107 plus 38 others) will have accumulated deficits in five years equal to their present liquid assets. In ten years seventeen more institutions will be in this unenviable position.

In other words, if they continued to operate as usual, within ten years 162 accredited four-year private colleges and universities in this study—or, by simple extrapolation, 223 in the entire nation —will run deficits equal to or exceeding their present liquid assets. This is equivalent to saying that within ten years 30 percent of all private Bachelor's institutions and Limited Master's institutions, 20 percent of the Master's institutions, and nearly 25 percent of all Ph.D. granting colleges and universities could be ready to go out of business. Half of all the private colleges in the Mountain region could be eligible for this ultimate solution as well as 43 percent of those in the West North Central region, 35 percent of those in the Pacific region, and 32 percent in the West South Central region. By enrollment levels: 32 percent of the Smallest, 36 percent of the Small, 27 percent of the Medium, 21 percent of the Large, and 23 percent of the Largest.

Prospective Demise Based on 1971 Deficits

I repeated this analysis of deficit in relation to total liquid assets using updated 1971 projected figures, bearing in mind that final figures tend to be much worse ($27,000, or 26 percent, worse in 1970) than projected figures. The assumption was made that there was no increase in the total liquid assets reported at the close of fiscal 1969 unless the institution ran a surplus in either 1969 or in 1970. If it did, the surplus was added to its liquid assets. But if it ran a deficit in either or both of those years, that amount was subtracted from its liquid assets before analyzing its 1971 deficit in relation to its total liquid assets. This process enabled me to take advantage of the surpluses that most institutions still ran in 1969 and puts as happy a face on these 1971 data as possible.

The question "How many can last how long?" was asked only of institutions reporting anticipated deficits for 1971. If an institution reported that it expected a surplus—warranted or unwarranted—I took it at its word even if it had run deficits the two previous years and in the process had exhausted its total liquid assets. The result is a crude picture, to be sure, but probably a conservative one.

If private colleges and universities proved to run deficits in 1971 no greater than they had forecast, there would have been 122 from the study alone that would have run deficits equaling or exceeding their total liquid assets. If the actual figures for 1971 proved to be as much worse than projected figures as was true for 1970 projected and actual figures, the devastating effect would have been to add substantially to the number of institutions with zero years to go before running deficits exceeding their total liquid assets. Those running deficits and without liquid assets could scarcely avoid plunging into debt—further into debt, in most cases. This, occurrence in turn, would make it additionally difficult to improve their situation in subsequent years. When liquid assets go, institutional elasticity and good credit standing go also, and in their place comes additional debt service. The more exhausted the institution becomes, the greater the burden it is asked to support.

In addition to the 122 that could go zero more years, there were twenty-five colleges and universities that could continue some fraction of one year if the expected 1971 deficit repeated itself before running equal to or exceeding total liquid assets. Another sixty-seven could continue up to five years; and forty more could sustain deficits of this magnitude for five to ten years. Also, seven institutions hoping for balanced budgets in 1971 had already run deficits exceeding their liquid assets. Because they did not forsee an actual deficit, however, they were not included in the reckoning.

In all, there were 254 institutions in the study expecting deficits in 1971 that would have run deficits exceeding their total liquid assets under a policy of business as usual within ten years. Half of them had already depleted their liquid assets. The number of institutions out of a total of 762 private accredited four-year colleges and universities in the nation that may thus have been predicted to be running deficits equaling or exceeding their liquid assets within ten years was 365—one for every day of the year. Instead of naming the days for the births of saints, we can name them for the deaths of the colleges that are named for the saints.

Translated into percentages these figures mean that if nothing changed, two-thirds of all the private colleges and universities in the West North Central region—seven states in the geographical center of the country running south from Minnesota and the Dakotas to Missouri and Kansas—could be ready to go out of business in ten years. Forty percent of the colleges and universities in this region, according to their updated projections, had already run deficits exceeding their total liquid assets.

Over 60 percent of those in the Mountain region could be going within this ten year period. Over 50 percent of those in the West South Central and East South Central regions, and between 40 and 50 percent of those in the Pacific, East North Central, Mid-Atlantic, and New England regions would have run deficits exceeding their total liquid assets in ten years and be prospects for the undertaker. In the South Atlantic region "only" 36 percent would be so stricken.

In ten years that figure would have included 58 percent of all private doctor's universities, 16 percent of them having already run deficits exceeding their liquid assets. It would have included 50 percent of all bachelor's institutions and 45 percent of the limited master's institutions. It would have included 72 percent of the smallest institutions, 64 percent of all Roman Catholic–related institutions, 52 percent of Methodist-related colleges and universities, and 40 percent of those independent of church relationship. The demographic characteristics of these institutions is set forth in full detail in Table 4.

Will these colleges fold in the year in which they exhaust their liquid assets? No, not many. But how far below the zero line will thoughtful members of their boards of trustees let them go? How many years their creditors will let them go depends in part on how large their deficits are. One may presume that the days—not the years—are numbered for colleges and universities that run deficits which are 8 percent or more of their total operating budgets. In 1969 nearly 20 percent of the Smallest institutions did just that, and so did 16 percent of the Small, 8 percent of the Medium, 2 percent of the Large, and 5 percent of the Largest.

Even more impelling, perhaps, is the question "How much longer will their publics—alumni, donors, state and federal legislators—let them go before bringing them the kind of aid that is necessary for their survival?" The situation is getting worse, not better. For all of their brave talk, as a group they have not turned the corner. They cannot last indefinitely. Each follow-up study we make will be based upon fewer colleges unless more is done immediately to correct this fiscal imbalance.

Table 4. DEMOGRAPHIC CHARACTERISTICS OF 254 COLLEGES AND
UNIVERSITIES THAT WOULD HAVE EXHAUSTED THEIR TOTAL
LIQUID ASSETS WITHIN TEN YEARS IF EACH YEAR BROUGHT
A DEFICIT AS LARGE AS THEY EXPECTED IN 1971

	Number	Percentage of Total Number
Geographic Region		
Pacific	17	40
Mountain	5	63
West South Central	14	54
East South Central	20	57
West North Central	54	67
East North Central	50	46
South Atlantic	27	36
Mid-Atlantic	44	42
New England	22	48
Degree Level		
Bachelor's	163	50
Limited Master's	44	45
Master's	19	37
Limited Doctor's	6	30
Doctor's	2	58
Enrollment Level		
Smallest	21	72
Small	108	59
Medium	81	41
Large	16	26
Largest	28	47

Institutional Forecasts

In the course of seeking updated data, institutions were
asked a broadly phrased question about their fiscal future: "In
general, how does your prognosis for the financial future of your
institution in the next two years compare with your projection a
year ago?" They had five options ranging from much better to
much worse. As could be expected, the bulk (199) of those responding indicated that their future looked about the same to them
now as it did a year earlier. Slightly more (126)' expected 1972–74

to be better than those (110) that expected it to be worse; and twice as many (32) expected it to be much better than those (15) that expected it to be much worse.

I then referred to a categorization of these institutions based upon their net current fund surplus or deficit at the end of fiscal 1969 to see whether their experience that year affected their response to this question. Among institutions that ran deficits that year and in each range of deficit, there were more institutions that said the future looked better to them than it had a year ago than there were institutions that said it looked worse; but, among institutions that ran surpluses in 1969, in virtually every range of surplus, there were more institutions that said the immediate future looked worse than it had in the summer of 1970 than there were those that said it looked better.

Once again, better may not mean good—indeed it probably does not—and there is little basis for discovering in these answers whether in specific instances the optimistic response is warranted or unwarranted. These figures suggest, however, that many institutions that ran a deficit in 1969 began hauling in the reins so that 1972–1974 looked "better" to them than it had a year ago, while many institutions that ran surpluses in that year were no longer confident that the immediate future held as much promise as they thought it had a year ago.

Unhappily, when an institution reported that its financial future looked the same, this failed to differentiate two implicit responses: "the same—and bad" or "the same—and good." In a similar manner better and much better may still be bad but simply less bad than earlier anticipated. One has little way of knowing, moreover, how often the more optimistic response was warranted by concrete indicators and how often sustained only by hope. In view of other specific data, however, it may be safely concluded that better more often meant less bad than good.

Current State of Financial Affairs

What these responses and subsequent correspondence with the presidents and chief business officers in several of these institutions suggest is that some institutions have found—and have found the courage to deal with—fat in the institutional budget. They have

met, as Shylock did, the dilemma that you do not cut away the fat
without shedding some blood and trimming away some muscle.
The altogether useless and vestigial organs in the institutional body
are likely to be, like the appendix in the human body, relatively
small.

Some private institutions continue to evade the whirlpool of
current fund deficits. An attractive academic program, an identifiable constituency, favorable geographic location, good administration—and good fortune—all seem to play a role in the felicitous
condition of these institutions. Similarly, those institutions that are
making a comeback are working on as many of these fronts as possible. They are becoming better managers of both income and expenditures; they have sought to identify their student markets
specifically; and, above all, they are articulating attractive academic
programs. They are achieving a balanced budget by some expenditure cuts combined with continuing income and constant enrollment.

Yet some of the institutions that are struggling toward
or achieving a balanced budget are still in a precarious state.
They are juggling short-term budget cuts while walking a tight-
rope. An institution may, for instance, get by without any faculty
raises for one year, perhaps two. An increasing number of institutions are being forced to this exigency. In 1971–72, 9 percent
reported no increase or a decrease in faculty salaries. In 1972–73,
12.4 percent so reported. This may release funds to pay off some
high interest debts, or it may give the institution another year in
which to increase income by finding new sources or by increasing
enrollment. This breathing time may enable the institution to turn
the corner on its financial situation and hold it. It is a short-term
adjustment, however, and unless accompanied by permanent
change, it will not provide salvation. It is disconcerting to receive
reports of an improved financial picture from institutions that also
report lagging enrollment.

Numerous campus visits, spot checks, and regional meetings
undertaken since the first of these data were gathered require this
current appraisal: while finances appear generally better in the
short run, the prospects show no significant improvement in the
long run. A few institutions that rode above the sea of current fund
deficits in the late sixties and beginning of the seventies are now

experiencing their first deficit years. These are not badly managed institutions; their administrations, moreover, looked carefully at the assigned causes of the plight of their neighbors. But they have still been unable to avoid experiencing the same difficulties.

The present situation of many colleges running deficits during the years covered by this study is best summarized in a letter I received recently. His college, my correspondent wrote, is not quite as close to the end as it seemed to be a year ago, thanks to the half million dollar surgery performed on it, "but the situation is still critical and prospects are not much better." The letter goes on to outline a deepening deficit, an increase in tuition, a further freeze on salaries, as well as a fragile increase in applications, which, together with better support from alumni and parents, rekindles hope on his campus.

Part of what we seem to be experiencing currently in the relevation of college finances may be likened to the degree of decolletage permitted in women's fashions in different eras. It is no longer quite as acceptable to expose the cleavage between current fund income and current fund expenditure as it was during a brief and welcome period of honesty. More, this separation itself is less acceptable than it was. A flattening out has been demanded wherever possible even at the expense of attractiveness. Reputation today hinges on a prim appearance.

The sober refusal to let expenditures outstrip income is, by and large, welcome. Although in some instances an institution ought to run a current fund deficit, these ought to be planned deficits. What appears to me to be unwelcome is a growing reticence in some institutions to share openly the fact of their financial need. The latent constituencies of many of these institutions need to be further aroused. The institutions can be saved. They ought to be. What their constituencies need to know is that the colleges can be saved if their supporters continue to act in concert.

As a reviewer of the financial status of private institutions, I feel most uneasy about their financial prospects when looking at current and anticipated enrollments. One of the principal factors in the financial past and future of private higher education is enrollment. Growth has been a justifier; decline is an accuser. A detailed review of what has been happening in enrollments in private colleges and universities is in order.

Enrollment Patterns

We asked the institutions in this study to report on past and projected enrollment patterns. We sought to obtain information for every year from 1965–66 through 1971–72 (hereafter simply 1965 and 1971) on freshman applications, freshman admissions, freshman head count enrollment, total undergraduate head count enrollment, total graduate head count enrollment, total full-time equivalent undergraduate enrollment and total full-time equivalent graduate enrollment. This was a formidable request for an enormous amount of data. Not surprisingly, some of the respondents quailed before the task. What is surprising is the very substantial number that were able to supply all of these data.

It is also interesting to note the points at which the largest number of willing but unable respondents fail. Freshman applications and freshman admissions are not, apparently, such generally accepted categories that all colleges and universities maintain careful and easily accessible records on them. Seventy-two institutions (13 percent) were unable to supply data on their freshman applications in 1965, and eighty-one institutions (15 percent) were unable to state how many freshman applicants they granted admission in that year. Only twenty-nine institutions (5 percent) were unable to supply freshman head count enrollment for 1965, and less than 3 percent failed to supply total head count and total full-time equivalent data for that year. The data were better for 1966 but some of that year's data were still too entangled in the cobwebs of history for 10 or 12 percent of sample institutions. Although as many as 8 or 9 percent of the institutions in some of the remaining years found data on freshmen too much of a nuisance to report, beginning with 1967 the responses improved considerably.

Until 1971. Eleven percent declined to project any enrollment data—not merely freshman data—for that year. Fourteen percent declined to speculate on freshman applications and 17 percent on freshman admissions. It is fascinating but unproductive to imagine the reasons for omitting projected enrollment data for 1971. Perhaps some looked into the crystal ball, did not like what they saw and, to avoid giving the image permanency in their minds, did not record it. No doubt most of those declining to answer thought that the shreds of evidence they had were too slender for the projection of these kinds of data.

There are many ways to report these data but none of them, alas, is fully satisfactory. If we reduce all of the figures to a per reporting institution basis and develop percentages from that point, we have no control over the nature of the institutions that pop in and out of the data, reporting where they have information and absenting themselves from the statistics when they do not. On the other hand, to reduce the data entirely to institutions which were able to respond to all forty-nine items on enrollment would lower the response rate more than necessary and make a special selection among the total number of institutions about which we could know little and over which we would have no control. Is there, for example, a relationship between the fact that an institution is unable to supply certain data for 1965 and its financial condition? Perhaps, but there is no way of knowing.

What we have done, therefore, is to eliminate from any category—freshman applications, for instance—institutions unable to supply data for all the years. Because a smaller number of institutions are able to supply data on freshman admissions—to take another for instance—we reduce the data to a "per reporting institution" basis when making comparisons between categories. Because this method also includes the possibility that the data are skewed in hidden ways, comparisons between categories may be more suggestive than precise.

Reluctantly excluding, then, all institutions that failed to supply freshman application data in any one year, the text discusses the application picture that emerges for 431 private colleges and universities—80 percent of our respondents—from 1965 through a projected 1971.

Freshman Applications

Freshman applications decreased mildly in 1966, declined again the following year, and held without increase until 1969 when they increased 4.6 percent. This lent courage to private institutions and they projected a further 4.6 percent increase in 1970 to be followed by a still greater increase for 1971. From 1965 through 1971, this is a cumulative increase of 13.6 percent, only 2.8 percent of which had actually been realized at the time the data were reported. The remainder was projected to come in the next two years.

Freshman applications are needed, of course, to produce freshman admissions from which come freshman enrollments, which contribute in turn to total enrollment, and this needs to rise to conform to the long-range plan and to balance the projected budget, or at least reduce its imbalance. This is very logical and very hopeful. Logic and hope, however, do not produce increased freshman applications.

In 1967, when freshman applications declined, private colleges and universities reacted by raising their percentages of admissions, and still suffered a decline in freshman head count enrollment. Total undergraduate head count enrollment—thanks, apparently, to transfers and better retention, actually increased.

The zero percent change in freshman applications in 1968 prompted the extension of the strategem employed the previous year. Accordingly, private institutions again raised their rate of admissions, admitting almost 60 percent of the freshmen who applied. The ploy was not altogether successful, however, for freshman head count enrollment actually increased only trivially. In 1969 freshman applications increased, the percentage admitted stayed at about 60 percent, and, as an apparent consequence, freshman head count enrollment increased.

As respondents looked to the fall of 1970 they saw a further increase in freshman applications, a slight fall in the rate of admissions, with a net gain in freshman head count and in total undergraduate enrollment. In making predictions for the fall of 1971, however, these institutions had their eyes more on their budget needs than on their recent application-admission-enrollment history. Freshman applications were projected to rise again handsomely; the rate of freshman admissions was projected to return to a rate just under that employed in 1968; and freshman head count, total undergraduate head count, and total undergraduate full-time equivalent were all projected to rise again.

For institutions with a cumulative percentage increase of 10.3 percent in total head count enrollment over the five years of data covered by the years 1965 through 1970, a projected rise in 1971 of slightly less than 3 per cent does not seem unreasonable or overly ambitious; except that over the five years of known data the percentage of increase had declined each succeeding year until in 1970 it was less than 1 percent. Like the merchants in Herb Shriner's hometown who, anxious for tourist trade, lowered the speed limit to zero and then passed a law against backing up, private colleges seemed to be trying by an act of will to determine that enrollment would rise.

Using data only from institutions able to supply information for all of the years from 1965 through 1971 eliminates a number of institutions whose ability to predict may be less precise than that of other institutions, partly because of an inadequate history of data. If we included in the 1971 projections those institutions eliminated because of an inadequate history of data, the hoped-for increase would be 7.6 percent rather than the 5.7 percent noted in the table below. Institutions with the most inflated expectations regarding future enrollment patterns often appear to be also the ones with inadequate data.

The more discouraging the past data and the more perilous the present situation, the higher the expectations for the future. This is evident when the patterns of institutions by various enrollment

Table 5. ENROLLMENT TRENDS FOR PRIVATE INSTITUTIONS
SHOWING YEAR-TO-YEAR PERCENTAGE CHANGES, 1966–1971

	Freshman Applications	Percentage of Freshmen Admitted	Freshman Head Count	Total Undergraduate Head Count
1966	−0.3	+1.1	−2.3	+3.6
1967	−1.5	+1.6	−1.3	+2.5
1968	0.0	+1.6	+0.4	+1.5
1969	+4.6	+0.1	+3.2	+0.7
1970 (anticipated)	+4.6	−1.2	+3.4	+1.6
1971 (anticipated)	+5.7	−0.8	+4.4	+2.9

groups are compared. An examination of the percentage of increase
or decrease in freshman applications from one year to the next is
highly revealing.

Large institutions appeared to have, collectively, a more
realistic view of future freshman applications in the light of their
past record than any other group. The expectations of the Largest
institutions also seemed relatively sober in the light of previous
performance. And the expectations of the group of institutions in the
Medium range, while high, appeared relatively reasonable when
compared with institutions in the Small range, let alone when compared with the Smallest.

For all enrollment groups save one, both 1966 and 1967
were years in which freshman applications decreased. That one
group—the group of institutions having the largest enrollments—
experienced a mild decline in freshman applications only in 1968.
No group could afford to take a decline in freshman applications
smilingly and probably none did, but the group with the least occa-
sion for smiling was the group of Smallest institutions. They experienced, successively, a 5.8 percent decrease and then a further
12.5 percent decrease. The rate of decrease declined the following
year to only 1.4 percent. This halted what must have seemed like
the pull of gravitational acceleration, but it was scant comfort.

However, the following year—1969—was a year of recovery

for all five enrollment groups. The group of Largest institutions received a much increased number of freshman applications, compensating not only the decrease of the year before but the decelerated rate of increase of the year before that. The group of Large institutions repeated its increase of the year before and thereby overcame the losses of the previous two years. The group of Medium institutions experienced a handsome increase of 5 percent which complemented the smaller increase of the year before.

Only the two smallest enrollment groups did not make sufficient recovery in applications for 1969 to exceed the numbers of applications they had received in 1965. The Small institutions followed three years of 3 and 4 percent declines by a 2 percent increase in 1969, while the Smallest received a whopping 8.3 percent increase. Coupled with the previous heavy losses noted above, however, this still left a net loss since 1965 of 12 percent.

The following two years of data are based on projections submitted by the individual institutions themselves. As already noted, the larger institutions, with projections varying from 2.0 to 3.7 percent, did not let one year of improvement carry them away in their projections. The same does not appear to be true for the smaller institutions (enrolling 2000 or less) whose projected increases ranged from 6.3 to 21.5 percent.

While no one looking at application data from 1965 through 1968 would have been likely to predict the 8.3 percent increase in 1969 which institutions in the Smallest category actually experienced—and this lent pause to too ready criticism of their collective expectations—nevertheless, the prediction of another 8.3 percent increase to be followed by a 21.5 percent increase does take one's breath away. Once over Niagara on an innertube is remarkable. To be followed by a repeat performance and this in turn to be capped by a ride down the Victoria Falls seemed incredible.

What these institutions were doing, of course, was probably less prediction than translation. The budget was being translated into the enrollment increases that had to be achieved if the budget projections were to be met. Percentage changes of considerable magnitude come easy where small numbers are involved. A small college looks ahead and hopes for a few more students. Yet, examined as a percentage and in light of previous performance, seeking those few additional students becomes a task of very large proportions. As shadows thrown on the wall, these percentages cast a sobering if somewhat exaggerated image over their plans and prospects.

Applications and Applicants

The decline in freshman applications at many private institutions has often been attributed to fewer applications per student. Each contemporary student is presumed to be filing applications with fewer colleges than his counterpart did formerly. This is a comforting doctrine and in local instances certainly has validity. It is, moreover, likely to become a more prevalent practice as students begin to realize that there are enough openings in higher education to make it unnecessary to file multiple applications in order to insure admission somewhere. However, the doctrine can be a two-edged sword, cutting in more than one direction. A decline in applications may not represent a decline in applicants; but an increase in applications, by the same token, may not represent an increase in applicants.

A precise applications-to-applicants ratio that will fit neatly into our data does not exist. Both Educational Testing Service and the American College Testing Program have data on the number of institutions to which tested candidates want their scores sent; but for a whole catalog of reasons, these cannot be made to conform to our data with sufficient precision to justify their use. Even small imprecisions can result in large distortions when a ratio of applications per applicant is applied to hundreds of thousands of applications.

However, three of the annual profiles of college freshmen published by the American Council on Education contain information that can be used to speak to this point. Students who were freshmen in the fall of 1967, 1968, and 1969 were asked how many applications they made to other institutions. From their responses, one can arrive at an average number of applications per student. (Grouping the American Council data into a single private college and university category provides a rough ratio of applications to applicants that is useful for analyzing the numbers of applications received by all private institutions in this study even though these data, covering but three years, permit only two comparisons—although these three years are important ones—and only in a limited way.) By applying this average number of applications per freshman student to the freshmen applications which the surveyed institutions reported receiving in those years, there is some basis for judging whether the percentage changes in applications received are themselves significant or are substantially affected by the numbers of applications freshmen send. One hundred applications might be generated by twenty-five applicants sending four each. Seventy-five applications received the next year might be a significant 25 percent drop; or it might be due to the fact that the same number of applicants are sending only three applications apiece, or that twice as many applicants are averaging one and one-half applications each.

The freshmen who enrolled in private institutions in the fall of 1967 in four categories used in the American Council studies—private four-year nonsectarian, Protestant four-year, Catholic four-year, private university—collectively averaged 2.60 applications per student. Those who enrolled in the fall of 1968 averaged 2.73 applications each, and those who enrolled in the fall of 1969 averaged 2.69 each.

By applying these ratios to the total number of applications received by our reporting institutions we discover that the zero percentage change in applications between 1967 and 1968 was actually a 4.8 percent decrease in numbers of applicants while the 4.6 percent increase in 1969 over 1968 was really better—a 6.2 percent increase in the actual number of applicants.

Also available is a breakdown between independent, Roman Catholic, and Protestant institutions as well as a category for private universities. Unfortunately, none of the religious groupings in this study—independent, Catholic, Protestant—is limited to four-year institutions. They include "universities" as well. Moreover, American Council data are received from freshmen actually enrolled in an institution identified in one of these three ways. It is by no means certain that if a given freshman submitted two other applications that these were to institutions of the same type. However, these cross-overs may tend to cancel one another. With these caveats in mind, some sub-analyses may still offer illumination on a dark problem.

The applicant-applications ratio has not been the same for these three groupings. It has fallen for those institutions independent of church relationship, although their applicant-applications ratio is still highest; risen for those related to the Roman Catholic Church; and first rose, then fell, for institutions related to Protestant denominations, whose applicant-applications ratio is lowest.

When these ratios are applied to the numbers of applications these types of institutions received and are compared with percentages of change in numbers of applications received from one year to the next, some striking observations may be made. A comparison of applications received in one year with applications received the next understates the increase in actual applicants for independent institutions, understates the severity of the decline for Roman Catholic-related institutions in 1968, and contradicts the slight rise for these institutions in 1969; and understates both the decline and the subsequent rise for Protestant-related institutions.

The following table depicts these numbers and percentages of change between years.

The category "university" is not one employed in this study, which differentiates rather among institutions by degree level and extent of the graduate program. Institutions offering doctoral programs in three areas or less, for instance, are distinguished from those offering the doctorate in four or more areas. However, we can roughly approximate the term as used by the Office of Education, on which the American Council study relies. The applications-to-applicants ratio varies only very slightly for private universities over the three year period—2.97, 3.07, 3.01—but when applied to the numbers of applications, it suggests a considerably modified picture. In terms of raw numbers of applications received, 1968 varied only slightly from 1967—a 0.3 percent increase; yet the actual number of applicants appears to have dropped 3.0 percent. Between 1968 and 1969 the number of applications increased 6.7 percent while the actual number of applicants increased 8.9 percent. In other words, the virtually unchanged numbers of applications received in the first two years masks the fact that a drop in actual

Table 6.   NUMBER OF APPLICATIONS AND APPLICANTS RECEIVED
BY PRIVATE INSTITUTIONS: 1967–1969

	Applications Received by Colleges and Universities	Average Number of Applications per Freshman	Derived Actual Number of Applicants	Percentage Change in Applications	Percentage Change in Applicants
Independent					
1967	242,755	3.2	75,861	0.2	6.9
1968	243,235	3.0	81,078		
1969	259,903	2.9	89,622	6.9	10.5
Catholic					
1967	108,239	2.2	49,200	−0.5	−8.8
1968	107,680	2.4	44,867		
1969	109,071	2.5	43,628	1.3	−2.7
Protestant					
1967	156,182	2.1	74,372	−0.06	−8.7
1968	156,093	2.3	67,867		
1969	161,598	2.2	73,454	3.53	8.2

applicants had taken place, while the increase in applications the third year understates the larger increase in actual applicants.

Individual colleges, of course, are still without a basis for analyzing their own applications-to-applicants ratio. Unless they have made this kind of study among their own students, they will have no way of knowing even if the norm for their type of institution applies to them. History, moreover, is no sure guide to the precise interpretation of the present. What may be useful to individual colleges, however, is the combined comfort and warning evident in the analysis above: a decrease in applications may not reflect a decrease in real applicants; but an increase in applications may be equally deceptive. It is a frail instrument for the admissions officer to use in gauging his progress from one year to the next or for reporting to his president on the admissions status of the institution.

Admissions and Freshman Enrollment

The "yield" (the rate at which applying freshman students found acceptable to the institution are translated into actual freshman enrollment) declined significantly for the national sample over the years covered by these data. The percentage of freshman students who, after being admitted by the institutions, actually showed up declined progressively from 66 percent in 1965 to 65 percent in 1966, then to 62 percent, 61 percent, 60 percent in 1969, and was projected to stay at the 60 percent level for the next two years.

Among institutions classified by size of enrollment, the group of institutions with the best record of translating admissions into actual enrollment is the group of Smallest institutions. In 1965 these institutions translated 76 percent of the freshmen they admitted into actual enrollment. That rate tumbled downward over the next few years to 73, 71, 70, and 67 percent.

The group doing the poorest job of translating freshman admissions into freshman head count enrollment is the Largest. From 62 percent in 1965 to 60 percent the following two years, to 59 percent in 1968, the rate dipped to 57 percent in 1969. The Small institutions, dropping from 72 to 62 percent, have a pattern which resembles that of the Large institutions which fell from 70 to 63 percent while the Medium group with a steady decline from 66 to 60 percent has a pattern more like that of the group with the largest enrollments.

Again, the groups suffering the most marked change are the two smallest enrollment groups. Although these two groups remained more successful in 1969—by five and ten percentage points severally—in translating freshman admissions into freshman enrollment than the group with the largest enrollments, their grip on this translation rate has weakened by nine and ten percentage points while the group with the largest enrollments has lost only five. All groups are on stormy seas but the pitch of the waves is steepest for the smallest institutions.

There are several possible variables at work in this phenomenon of declining yield. One might expect that, if admitted, an applicant would accept the invitation of his first choice. His first choice need not be prestigious; it is enough that it is his first choice. But if the student aid package is not sufficient for his wants, he may decline the invitation of his first choice and go where the net cost to him is less. These two variables, perceived prestige and net cost, probably have been active, sometimes in consort, sometimes in opposition, in bringing about the decline in freshman yield in private institutions.

In 1965 freshmen constituted 28.4 percent of the total undergraduate head count enrollment in private institutions. Their percentage of the whole has declined in the intervening years to 26 percent. While this makes for a somewhat more even spread among the undergraduate classes, it also means that there has been a decline in the segment of undergraduates which is relatively less expensive than the remaining segments. In the typical undergraduate program, freshmen cost less to educate than upperclassmen. They are frequently concentrated in larger classes as they fulfill common distribution requirements. Upper level courses in a student's major field, tutorials, independent study—all more expensive and less easy to program than beginning survey or distribution courses— come later.

The advantage of a high ratio of freshmen to total undergraduate enrollment has a counterbalancing disadvantage, especially in very small schools, in the large number of small classes run at the upper level that could accommodate more students at no greater instructional cost to the college. Even so, the drop in the percentage that freshmen compose of the entire student body in very small institutions may be partly responsible for, or reflect, the severity of their fiscal problem. The pattern of freshmen as a percentage of total enrollment between the fall of 1965 and the fall of 1970 for the enrollment groups has been as follows:

Smallest declined 6.7 percentage points from 34.0 to 27.3
Small   declined 6.3 percentage points from 34.8 to 28.5
Medium declined 2.3 percentage points from 30.8 to 28.5
Large   declined 2.2 percentage points from 26.7 to 24.5
Largest declined 0.5 percentage points from 22.4 to 21.9

The reader familiar with statistics dealing with the attrition problem may be troubled at this point. If only forty percent of the entering freshmen at a given college graduate on schedule (four years after matriculation) and only 20 percent more graduate eventually from some college, that still leaves a dropout rate of 40 percent. Since in these circumstances it is unlikely that any of the other classes will be larger than the freshman class, how can these attrition figures be reconciled with figures that show freshman enrollment to be but a quarter—or less—of total undergraduate enrollment?

First of all, we asked the institutions replying to our survey to respond according to Office of Education Higher Education General Information Survey (HEGIS) practice. This means that only students who are enrolled in higher education for the first time directly following high school should be identified in these data as freshmen. In terms of class standing, there are many students who are not freshmen in this pristine sense, yet who at the same time are not sophomores. They are incoming transfers with less than a year of transferable credit or freshmen from the previous year who did not achieve sophomore standing. These would be included in the total undergraduate figure, but not in the freshman figure. Our data are comparable to HEGIS data. According to Office of Education figures for all colleges and universities for fall 1970, first time degree credit students—i.e., "freshmen"—constitute, on a head count basis, 23.5 percent of the total undergraduate degree-credit enrollment.

Basic to a resolution of this apparent riddle is the realization that in this study we are not following a given class of students through their academic career. What we have is an aggregation of data from individual institutions and what we are comparing is any year's freshman with all other undergraduates. This masks a lot of in and out migration.

Many institutions seek to pick up as many or more transfers, from junior colleges and elsewhere, as they lose from their entering freshman class. The extent to which institutions, individually or collectively, achieve this goal is not visible in the figures available to us. Since our figures are for private institutions only, moreover, the migration of students between tax-supported and private institutions is lost to view.

There may be, furthermore, a beguiling temptation to think of the freshman class as one of only four classes and its percentage of the whole as one of four percentages that make up the 100 percent total. All of the students who take a fifth year—or at least more than four years—to earn a baccalaureate degree are hidden in the undergraduate total. While this group is unlikely to be large enough to constitute a fifth class, it is large enough to "put a little English" on the phenomenon.

Because we are not following a group of specific individuals, there is a delayed reaction that is not accounted for in these data. A drop in freshman enrollment in relation to total enrollment may be due to better retention of previous classes, as well as to incoming transfers, or to an actual drop in entering freshmen. If the drop is an actual decrease in freshmen, this will have its effect upon subsequent classes, not on previous classes already attending the institution.

Finally, the attrition rates cited above are for all of higher education, public and private. In some states the tax-supported institution is required to accept any applicant with a high school diploma. If the institution makes no adjustment in its curricular program, it may be expected to have a higher dropout rate than the private institution which is able to do more by way of selecting students for their presumed ability to succeed in college. The attrition rate for private four-year colleges and universities as a whole is not likely to be as high as for all of higher education.

Total Enrollment

The proof of the pudding is in actual total enrollment. After the freshman applications, the application-to-applicants ratio, and the rate of admissions, come the important figures: the number that actually enroll, and the number that stay enrolled.

As mentioned earlier, the rate of increase in total head count enrollment dropped steadily for private colleges and universities after 1965. Putting aside optimistic projections for 1970 and 1971, it is important to note that this declining rate of increase came during a period of rising rate of increase—at least until the fall of 1969 —for higher education as a whole, public and private, four-year and two-year. If enrollment in all higher education had not been increasing during this period, these small increases in enrollment in private institutions would probably have been actual decreases. Quite apart from the fact that all of higher education may be looking forward to a virtually static situation, and private higher education to a static or retrenching position, to have experienced a declining rate of increase in the midst of a rising rate for others is to have experienced something very much like an absolute decline. A declining situation is very different from a dynamic one both from a psychological and, apparently, from a cost point of view.

For some institutions it was not merely a declining rate of increase. It was an absolute decline. In the states of Alabama, Iowa, Maryland, and Wisconsin, for instance, private institutions suffered net losses in enrollment in 1969 over 1965; and in Kentucky, Louisiana, Missouri, and Nebraska, private institutions fell below their fall 1966 enrollments.

The regional picture softens the starker outline of difference among states but it still reflects these differences and in summary form it reveals that the enrollment scene is not identical around the country. While no region ends up, as four individual states do, with a net loss in undergraduate head count enrollment in 1969 over 1965, four of the regions reveal a stunted and declining enrollment growth. These are the regions that run straight through the geographic middle of the country. What makes this all the more striking is the fact that all four of these regions made large initial increases in 1966 over 1965.

Full-time equivalent enrollment is a somewhat imprecise category. Institutions were reminded to use for our survey the definitions employed when supplying information for HEGIS, but the method of arriving at a full-time equivalent may well have varied from one campus to another. Our data simply reflect the information supplied by each institution. By whatever method calculated, it is, of course, a device to get behind head count figures made up of full-time and part-time students to see what these figures would be if all part-time students could be regrouped to resemble full-time students. From an educational point of view it is important to know the head count figure, to know how many actual persons are being accommodated in higher education. From a financial point of view, full-time equivalent figures are generally more useful.

The percentage relation between subsequent years of full-time equivalent data is similar—and sometimes very nearly equal—to head count relationships, as Table 7 shows.

The year of greatest increase for each enrollment group in the study—and thus for all institutions combined—is the earliest year for which we have data to compare with the previous year.

Table 7. Undergraduate Enrollment: Head Count and
Full-Time Equivalent Percentage Increases: 1965–1970

	Head Count	Full-Time Equivalent
1965/1966	3.6	4.9
1966/1967	2.5	2.7
1967/1968	1.5	2.1
1968/1969	0.7	0.8
1969/1970	1.6 (projected)	1.5 (projected)
1970/1971	2.9 (projected)	2.7 (projected)

In the fall of 1966, full-time equivalent rose by 4.9 percent for all institutions combined. The smallest gain was 4.2 percent for institutions in the Large enrollment group and the largest gain—7 percent —was netted by the Smallest enrollment group.

The following year, 1967, the positions flipped. The enrollment group with the lowest rate of increase the previous year became the group with the highest increase simply by being the group whose percentage slipped the least. The group with the highest percentage of increase the previous year plummetted to the lowest increase the following year.

One year following, this Smallest enrollment group dropped still further to an actual net decrease in full-time equivalent enrollment. Changes of this magnitude, even if alleviated by later increases, have a violent impact on both the educational program and the economy of the small institution. As crash dieters have found, alternate quick gains and swift losses are far less healthy than weight stability. The problem is that this is good advice for the affluent man who—if he has the will—has considerable control over his increases or decreases, but poor advice for the impoverished who must take his feast or famine as these present themselves. Very small institutions, continually on the hunt for enough students to support a viable academic program, must accept all that a good hunt produces one year to make up for the losses of a previous or subsequent year.

For all institutions combined, the rate of increase in full-time equivalent enrollment has been a rapidly declining one. These figures are set forth in the table which follows.

The enrollment fortunes of these same institutions when examined by degree levels are also set forth in Table 8. There are variations in the patterns of separate groups, but, in general, their similarities are more striking than their differences.

The full-time undergraduate enrollment examined by geographical regions reveals uneven patterns. The Pacific and New England areas are different from the others and the eight institutions comprising the Mountain region again present a wildly careening pattern of ups and downs which hints at patterns for individual institutions or other very small groups of institutions. Larger groups have a smoothing effect on the statistical pattern. With large numbers of institutions even major changes appear mild, rather like riding a roller coaster with the brakes on.

1970 Follow-Up on Predictions

One year after the initial solicitation of data we asked private colleges and universities for updated information. This follow-up enabled us to see whether the predictions made a year earlier actually held up when the last student arrived and the final nose was counted.

While individual institutions often defy being taken captive by statistical averages, on the average the private institution failed to meet its projections.

There were some happy exceptions even among averages. For example, one region (East North Central) met and two regions (Pacific and New England) exceeded their forecast head count enrollment for 1970. All others fell short.

In all regions the forecast had been for increased enrollment over the previous year, even if enrollment had been dropping in previous years. In fact, in every region save one—West North Central—1970 was forecast to bring the highest enrollment since the base year, 1965. While, in five of the nine regions, 1970 did prove to be the highest enrollment to that point in time, in the West South Central and West North Central regions it was the lowest since 1965. In the West North Central, in fact, enrollment very nearly returned to the 1965 level.

Actual enrollment exceeded predictions in eight states and

Table 8. FULL-TIME EQUIVALENT ENROLLMENT PERCENTAGE OF CHANGE BETWEEN EACH INTERVENING YEAR: 1965–1971

	1965/66	1966/67	1967/68	1968/69	Anticipated 1969/70	Anticipated 1970/71
Enrollment						
Smallest	7.0	0.3	−1.3	1.4	7.9	11.7
Small	4.7	2.8	0.9	−1.0	1.5	4.5
Medium	5.3	1.4	1.5	0.5	1.8	3.1
Large	4.2	3.8	2.3	2.9	1.5	2.2
Largest	4.7	3.3	3.3	0.9	1.0	1.3
Degree Levels						
Bachelor's	5.5	2.2	1.9	−0.3	2.0	3.5
Limited Master's	5.7	3.2	1.7	1.9	2.3	2.6
Master's	2.5	2.9	0.3	1.7	0.4	1.7
Limited Doctor's	8.7	1.8	2.9	1.1	1.1	2.8
Doctor's	3.1	3.4	3.6	1.3	0.7	1.1
Geographic Regions						
Pacific	3.2	2.5	1.9	3.5	2.9	2.8
Mountain	6.3	2.9	11.7	−0.1	2.9	1.6
West South Central	4.5	1.0	1.5	0.2	2.7	3.7
East South Central	4.2	2.0	0.3	−1.4	3.5	3.9
West North Central	5.8	−1.0	0.1	−1.4	0.5	3.7
East North Central	5.3	2.2	0.9	0.0	1.6	2.1
South Atlantic	5.0	3.4	3.7	0.8	0.9	3.0
Mid-Atlantic	4.7	5.1	3.0	1.7	0.9	1.9
New England	2.2	2.8	0.7	3.2	1.7	2.1
All Institutions Combined	4.9	2.7	2.1	0.8	1.5	2.7

matched it in one. For the remainder, actual enrollments were lower than anticipated. In one state (Virginia) enrollment exceeded prediction by 8.1 percent, and in Washington by 3.6 percent. These were more than offset by states where enrollment reality fell short of projection by 9.6 percent (Maryland), 8.4 percent (Kentucky), 7.6 percent (Florida), 6.5 percent (Kansas), 5.6 percent (Nebraska), and 5.1 percent (South Dakota).

Enrollment for fall 1971 was, in turn, forecast to be even higher than that anticipated for 1970. In most cases, in fact, it was forecast to be much higher. It was as though some governor operated to restrain the expectation for the immediate fall that did not similarly restrain the optimistic expectations for a year hence. That governor, of course, was the information coming from the admissions office. Since that information could not be altogether ignored, a certain amount of realism tempered the predictions for the upcoming academic year. The need to project a reversal in the declining enrollment graph was so great, however, that recent experience was ignored and enrollment higher than ever was predicted for 1971. These expectations, like those for 1970, were to prove unrealistic.

Undergraduate enrollment decreased in private universities in 1971 by 1.5 percent and held for no gain in private four year colleges. In 1972 enrollment fell off still further in the private sector, declining 2.1 percent in private universities and 1.7 percent in private four year colleges. Furthermore, relying on the slender reed of applications data gleaned from spot checks around the country, one may say that while enrollment may actually increase in fall 1973 in an occasional rare state, it will barely hold its own in others, and will drop still further in most.

The institutions in our study taken as a national whole saw continuous growth in undergraduate head-count enrollment from 1965 to 1970. With each successive year, however, the increase grew less. As for a football team moving down the field, it became tougher and tougher to grind out yardage—and this in an era when enrollment in higher education was generally increasing. As the college-age cohort creeps down attempts to increase enrollment will get tougher still. Public institutions, to justify their heavy commitments to plant and program, are starting to make goal-line defenses of their enrollments that begin little short of mid-field.

It is striking to note that institutions without extensive graduate commitments (Limited Masters and Limited Doctors) did better in meeting their undergraduate expectations than those engaged more substantially in graduate work at either the masters or doctors level. For Doctors institutions, the decrease in undergraduate enrollment was accompanied by a substantial (11 percent) increase in graduate head count enrollment. At a time when federal support for graduate programs is at a low ebb, this decrease in undergraduate enrollment coupled with an increase in graduate enrollment will have adverse effects on the fiscal status of most of these institutions.

When analyzed by enrollment size, the data show that only the Largest institutions actually declined in undergraduate head count enrollment. All other groups increased. The group of Large institutions came closest to meeting its (modest) predicted increase. Paradoxically, although the group of Smallest institutions fell farthest short of meeting its anticipated increase, this group nevertheless had the largest increase over the preceeding year. Their reach far exceeded their grasp, but exceptional effort must have been put forth to attain the dramatic increase actually achieved.

The picture is not radically altered when one turns from undergraduate head count to full-time equivalent enrollment. By regions, the observable differences are West South Central—which is doing better on a full-time equivalent basis than on a head count basis—and South Atlantic, which is doing worse. In the enrollment groups, only the two largest show a difference between head count and full-time equivalent performance. By degree level groupings only the Limited Masters group performed noticeably different in 1970 by full-time equivalent from the way its performance shows up by head count. It exceeded its full-time equivalent projection; but fell short of its head count projection.

Graduate Enrollment

In the years covered by the study the big increase in graduate enrollment came in 1966. The graduate head count increase over the previous year was 6.9 percent. The total full-time equivalent graduate count rose 7.5 percent. This was in the same year that freshman head count enrollment decreased 2.3 percent and total undergraduate head count increased 3.6 percent.

It is probably just as well for private higher education that this rate of increase in graduate students did not sustain itself. It did continue to increase, however, at rates considerably higher than undergraduate increases for the following three years. Graduate head count enrollment increased by 4.6, 3.2, and 5.0 percent while full-time equivalent graduates progressed at rates of 5.4, 3.1, and 4.8. Then, suddenly, graduate enrollment headed for a decline: graduate head count to a 2.7 percent rate of increase and full-time equivalent to 1.7 percent. In the following year, 1971, these rates were expected to make a recovery of some lost ground with rates of increase of 3.1 and 3.6 percent respectively. If the projections proved accurate, this would mean a cumulative increase of 29 percent full-time equivalent graduates compared to a cumulative increase of 15.5 percent full-time equivalent undergraduates over the same time period.

Institutions in the Largest enrollment category—those enrolling more than 4000 students—account for as much as seven-eighths of all graduate students enrolled in private higher education, but the cumulative increase over these seven years of data for full-time equivalent graduate students in these institutions is only 22.8 percent. The really large graduate student increases were made by a score of institutions in the Large enrollment range (71.7 percent) and some two dozen institutions in the Medium range (76.2 percent).

In other words, although they account for only one-eighth of the graduate students—largely, but not entirely, at the masters degree level—their cumulative rate of increase was so high that the rate of increase for all private institutions combined (29 percent) is higher than the rate of increase for those institutions enrolling seven-eighths of the graduate students (23 percent).

Full-time equivalent graduate enrollment as a percentage of total full-time equivalent enrollment (on a per reporting institution basis) rose slightly in each of the years covered by the study from 29.7 percent in 1965 to 31.9 percent in 1969. It was projected to remain steady for the following two years. As long as the rate of increase in graduate students remains higher than the rate of increase in undergraduate students, then the proportion of graduate students to total enrollment will continue to rise. This appears to be what is happening. This may have adverse implications for the financial picture. Some graduate education, however, costs relatively little to provide. Full classrooms of students pursuing a masters degree in education are much healthier financially than many of the upper division undergraduate courses that operate with small enrollments. Graduate head count enrollment that was projected to increase in 1970 at a modest 2.7 percent and to accompany a 1.6 percent undergraduate head count enrollment increase, actually increased 6.2 percent while undergraduate enrollment fell off to a 0.5 percent increase.

Concluding Comment

Rarely does anyone attempt to describe a college or university without considering the students who study there. Many—and that includes more than students—say that the students are the college. Every institution of higher learning takes students very seriously. They are the name of the game. For educational purposes enrollments and, therefore, the study of enrollment patterns are important.

Enrollments are also important fiscally. Buildings are constructed, programs are developed, faculties are hired, fixed expenditures are committed, all on the basis of present and expected enrollment. An institution that builds plant and program for a student body that never reaches the expected size, or that rises and then falls, is apt to be in fiscal trouble, and its administrators may have some explaining to do. This is true in both tax-supported and private institutions.

If neither the percentage of college age students actually attending college nor the length of time they stay enrolled increases, while the college age population—which stands as proxy for postsecondary enrollments—heads toward a rate of increase near zero, both tax-supported and privately supported institutions will be scrabbling for students in order to justify their expanded plants and programs. This is already happening and does not make the admissions task of privately supported institutions any easier. An assembly of community junior college leaders, in the fall of 1972, advised its members to become much more involved in the active recruitment of students. The mere open door of the junior college has lured many potential students from the private campus. If junior colleges go out into the highways and byways and compel them to come in, the impact on enrollment in private institutions could be great.

All institutions are concerned with enrollments for both educational and fiscal reasons; but those that are dependent upon tuition and fee income for 40 percent of their total operating budget (nearly 50 percent of the total operating budget and close to 70 percent of the educational and general budget if sponsored research and medical center funds are excluded) are doubly concerned. (See Figure 4 in Chapter Four.)

In private institutions, not only are expenditure commitments made in the expectation that enough students will arrive to vindicate those commitments, but the students are expected to bring with them a substantial portion of the income necessary to sustain the commitments. In economic terms, tax-supported and privately supported institutions that make commitments beyond the number of arriving students are not different from one another. In either case, money is expended without yielding the expected benefit, and revenue is lost. The effect of miscalculation, however, is felt to a greater degree by the privately supported institution than by the tax-supported because the latter is not as dependent upon tuition income.

Moreover, since private institutions are more likely than tax-supported ones to be substantially residential in nature, a lower number of students than was expected adversely affects the income and expenditure pattern for auxiliary enterprises.

The study reported here shows that in all enrollment groups in our study except the Largest, auxiliary enterprises, especially residence halls, not only pay for themselves but actually generate net income which makes it possible for a college to provide, say, more student aid. In relation to auxiliary enterprises, a resident student is an asset. If he does not show up he is not merely a missing asset, he is a deficit. Debt service payments must be met on the space he would have occupied whether he shows up or not.

If the enrollment picture is to improve in private colleges and universities, many will need to be more aggressive in their pursuit of potential students, especially those beyond the 18 to 21 year old age group; they will also need to improve their performance in the retention of those who actually matriculate. To do these things they will need better data than many of them presently possess and better studies of where their students come from, why they come, and why they leave.

The pursuit and retention of students must begin with the clear articulation of an academic program that can meet the competition in meaning, purpose, and relevance. It continues when this message is carried by an admissions office which understands that its role is not counseling, first of all, but admission. It is carried further by a faculty which understands that a useful test of the smallness which it applauds is the rate of retention it is able to attain through the application of intimate concern.

The data which some institutions maintain in this critical area are sadly deficient. To judge by their ability to respond to our request for data, some institutions are overlooking areas where the need for precise data is important. To be without adequate data in an area as crucial as freshman admissions—the replenishment of the student body in both quality and quantity—is to treat casually an area of vital concern to the institution.

Even small miscalculations of what to expect of the future can have major effects on a small college. The unrealistic predictions made by a number of institutions in our study are partly the result of an inadequate history of data, and the insufficient analysis of what data they have. Unrealistic predictions lead to financial commitments which aggravate the fiscal imbalance.

More institutions need better studies of their students. They need to know where they come from geographically, economically, sociologically, and academically. They need to have studies that tell them, for example, that although the same amount of energy invested in two places elicits a comparable number of requests for admission, it produces two very different patterns of actual enrollment. They need to know a great deal more both about the students who do come and the ones who do not. They need to know how many applications their own students are filing, and have filed in the past.

In years when a smaller number of applicants are generating a larger number of applications, each institution may expect to be affected by the phenomenon by actually enrolling a smaller percentage of applicants than in years when more applicants generate fewer applications for admission. This is the statistical application of the phenomenon.

For the individual institution, however, each application does represent a real applicant. Whether it takes its statistical share of these students or improves it will depend upon how skillfully these applicants are handled. When the fishing is poor, a few fish may nibble on many lines. At times like these, the skill of the angler becomes critical.

If the enrollment picture in private colleges and universities is to improve, finally, more will have to be done within a state to bring about a more effective coordination of tax-supported and private institutions, including some reduction in the steadily widening gap between the two types of institutions in the charges levied directly on the student through tuition and fees.

The marked increase in college attendance is one of the most frequently cited reasons for the rising cost of higher education. This has had a greater influence on the public sector than on the private sector; private higher education's most recent financial stress is largely the result of other factors. Perversely, it is often the lack of an increase in enrollment or, in fact, an actual decrease in enrollment that has had the greater effect on private higher education. Much of private higher education could accommodate additional students with economic benefit.

The data in this chapter confirm what many have known: enrollment in private colleges and universities has fallen off and continues to decline. There are many complex reasons for this, including the two-price system which tags the educational garment at a higher price if purchased in a private institution than if purchased in a public one down the street. In some areas, the broad and rapid expansion of community colleges, undertaken with insufficient regard for existing institutions, has exacerbated this comparison. The reasons for the enrollment drop also include an apparent decline in servitude to the credentialing system which placed mystical as well as monetary value on a baccalaureate degree. They include the end of a military draft that formerly exempted those attending college. They include the current strong emphasis on vocationalism.

The fiscal implications of this enrollment decline are alluded to in the foregoing pages, but the theme is not belabored. If private higher education is to survive financially, it must also survive in enrollment. To accomplish this, both internal and external factors need to be improved. Private colleges and universities need good data, better analysis of data, aggressive admissions practices, and, above all, attractive academic programs. They also need external help if they are to be successful in their bid for students. Neither the institutions nor their students can continue to compete successfully against the quickening pace in the financial race while simultaneously leaping the ever-rising hurdles imposed by a dual pricing system which requires that one price be charged at one location while a much lower price is permitted elsewhere.

III

Where Does the Money Come From?

One of the questions that anyone interested in a particular private college wants answered is, "How does it compare in sources of income and expenditure with other private colleges?" There is something more than a little hazardous in applying information like this to a specific campus. For one thing, there are many different private colleges and universities serving different missions to different constituencies in different parts of the country. Their collective figures do not necessarily melt down to a normative standard for specific institutions. For another thing, the data upon which the answer is based are descriptions of what are, not what ought to be. The fact that "everybody else is doing it" has never been a very sure guide for action. Nevertheless, it is a place to start. We look first at sources of income.

To begin with a national picture, 68.1 percent of the educational and general revenue in private institutions is derived from tuition and fees. The second largest source of income is that received from restricted and unrestricted gifts and grants. They produce 15.3 percent of the whole. Income from endowment produces another 7.6 percent, contributed services is responsible for 1.7 percent, and all other sources for 7.3 percent.

If sponsored research and medical center revenues are added to the educational and general account, the percentages of the remaining items change considerably. If the national distribution of income and expenditures is to serve as a touchstone for smaller groups of institutions, however, the breakdown without sponsored research and medical center is probably more helpful.

There are objections to taking sponsored research and medical center revenues and expenditures out of the budget for purposes of comparison, even as there are objections to leaving them in. Presenting the data both ways offers further commentary on the differences that exist among private institutions. In examining the graphs which follow the reader will want to be aware of these differences. Take a single example, tuition and fee revenue. Two different orders and degrees of magnitude appear when private institutions, grouped in nine geographical regions, are first arranged in order of percentage of educational and general income derived from tuition and fees when sponsored research and medical center revenues are included, and then arranged in order when these sources are excluded. These two orders are set forth in the table below. Regions do not change more than two positions in the order, but the percentage derived from tuition and fee income changes as much as 24.4 percent. The major determinant in these percentage changes appears to be the extent to which the region is involved in medical education.

With sponsored research and medical center added to the revenue side of the ledger, the percentage contributed by tuition and fees becomes 51.2 percent, revenue to sponsored research contributes 12.8 percent, medical education ʼ(hospitals, schools, clinics, sponsored research) generates 12.0 percent, income from restricted and unrestricted gifts and grants becomes 11.5 percent, endowment income becomes 5.7 percent, contributed services 1.7 percent, and all other income 5.5 percent.

It is illuminating to make these same analyses when the institutions are grouped by enrollment levels. The Smallest institu-

Table 9. TUITION AND FEE INCOME AS A PERCENTAGE
OF EDUCATIONAL AND GENERAL REVENUES: 1969

Including Sponsored Research and Medical Center Income		Excluding Sponsored Research and Medical Center Income		Difference
East North Central	64.8	Mountain	75.3	12.4
Mountain	62.9	Mid–Atlantic	74.5	19.3
Mid–Atlantic	55.2	East North Central	74.1	9.3
Pacific	53.3	Pacific	69.7	16.4
West North Central	52.7	New England	63.9	14.8
West South Central	50.6	West South Central	62.9	12.3
New England	49.1	West North Central	60.9	8.2
East South Central	42.4	South Atlantic	60.2	24.4
South Atlantic	35.8	East South Central	59.4	17.0

tions depend more heavily than any other enrollment group upon contributed services and gifts and grants, derive the least percentage from endowment, and, like Small institutions, receive virtually no income for carrying on sponsored research. Medium institutions derive a larger percentage of income from tuition and fees and from endowment than any other enrollment group. The group of Large institutions leads the list in income from all other sources and is close to the leader in percentage of income derived from tuition and fees. (If sponsored research and medical center were included, however, tuition and fee income would be 10 percentage points less.) The Largest institutions received an insignificant amount from contributed services and their percentage of revenue from tuition and fees is close to that of the Small institutions. (With sponsored research and medical center included, however, tuition and fee income would drop approximately 25 percentage points.) Figure 3 exhibits these comparisons among sources of income.

Comparisons by degree levels indicate that Bachelor's, Limited Master's, and Master's institutions are all more dependent upon tuition and fee income than are universities offering the doctorate. Master's institutions at 75 percent are at the high end of the continuum while Doctors institutions at 60.4 percent are low. Limited Doctor's institutions derive the smallest percentage of educational and general income from endowment: Doctor's institutions, however, derive the largest. Contributed services make a rapidly diminishing contribution to revenue at each level of increasing institutional complexity. Institutions offering the masters degree derive the lowest percentage of income from gifts and grants. Those offering the doctorate derive the highest. These comparisons are set forth in Figure 3.

Tuition and Fee Income

Not only private colleges and universities but every kibitzer looking over their shoulders wonders how much more money—if any—can be eked out of tuition and fees. Like anxious farmers who need immediate income but must conserve the land for the long term, the colleges wonder whether they can plow and raise again their favorite cash crop or whether that land must be allowed to lie fallow. They would like to take the long view and not raise tuition every year lest they exhaust the resource, but their needs are immediate.

The ability of a private college or university to raise its tuition charges is contingent upon many things: the presumed quality of its education, the ability and willingness of prospective purchasers of its services to pay more, which in turn is dependent upon the rise in per capita income, the cost at which similar services may be obtained elsewhere, and so on. Such highly important aspects of the problem as the perception of quality among prospective purchasers lie outside the purview of this study. There are some aspects of data in this study, however, which may shed some illumination on the problem.

If it were not for the competition of the going market price and if the consumer of higher education engaged in cost benefit analysis, an institution deriving a relatively small percentage of its operating budget from tuition and fees might be able to increase its tuition income more than an institution already deriving a very large proportion of its operating budget from tuition. The logic for the hypothesis is that the student paying the smaller fraction of the cost of his education is receiving an education more highly subsidized from other sources and, perceiving that he is getting a better bargain for his money than the student whose tuition payments constitute a larger proportion of the cost of his education, would be

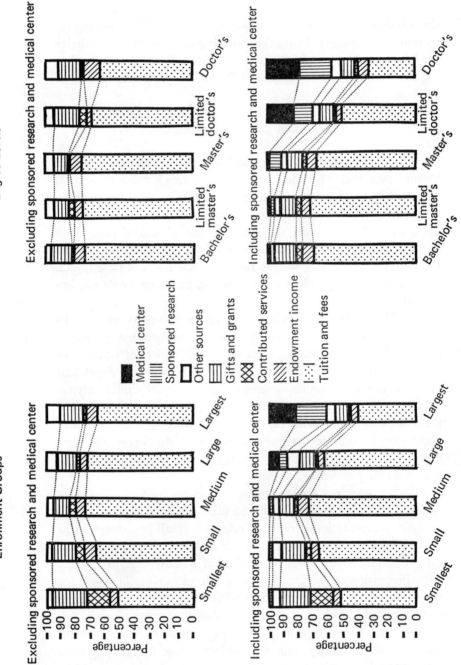

Distribution, educational and general account, 1969.

willing to pay more for it. However, the marketable product differences that an institution is able to exhibit may be less attractive to the potential student or his family than that of institutions deriving a higher percentage of their budgets from tuition. Thus, even though the institution was obtaining a small proportion of its operating budget from tuition and fees relative to other institutions, it would be limited in its ability to raise tuition further.

With this caveat in mind, it may still be instructive to look at the analytical grids to discover the variance, from one group to another, of tuition as a percentage of the cost of education.

Income from tuition and fees is a smaller contribution toward educational and general expenditures in institutions offering the doctorate than in institutions offering only lower degrees. In 1969, for example, tuition and fee income at Bachelor's and Limited Master's institutions supplied the income for three-fourths of their educational and general expenditures. The percentage supplied by tuition and fees decreases as the institution becomes more complex. At Master's institutions the percentage decreased to 70. At Limited Doctor's institutions, 54 percent. Finally, at Doctor's institutions the percentage dropped lower still to 35.

However, when medical center expenditures and sponsored research expenditures are dropped from all five categories (on the grounds that they produce offsetting revenues that in 1969 exceeded expenditures in these areas), the percentage differences among these types of institutions is considerably less marked.

Specifically, tuition and fee income contributes 74, 76, 76, and 72 percent of the educational and general expenditures (minus the two categories mentioned) for, respectively, Bachelor's, Limited Master's, Master's, and Limited Doctor's institutions. Only at Doctor's institutions does tuition and fee income contribute a percentage to educational and general expenditures that is noticeably different from its contribution at other institutions. At these complex universities the percentage is 63 percent.

If the economy grew equally on all fronts and consumer interest maintained its present distribution among alternative products, theoretically, tuition should be at least as expandable as a growing and inflating economy. Since students and their families presumably benefit from increased per capita disposable income along with the rest of the population, a tuition rise equivalent to the rise in per capita disposable income should be acceptable to the kind of student presently attending private institutions. If, as some prognosticators have forecast, average per capita income were to reach $15,000 by the turn of the century, why should tuition charges in private institutions not keep pace with such increases?

There are some problems with this theory, besides the vagaries of consumer satisfaction. We shall discuss only a few of them. One is that as tuition charges approach the cost of education received, the student gets less of a bargain than he did before and this makes the exchange less attractive. Institutions depending upon tuition and fee revenue for only 30 percent of their educational and general income do not have this problem to the same extent that institutions deriving 90 percent of their income from this source do. But as William Bowen and Hans Jenny and Richard Wynn have pointed out, tuition charges have been rising faster than real education costs. The continuing effect of this, it would seem, is to narrow the gap between what the student pays and the value he receives for his money.[1]

Another problem with the theory is that tuition has not merely kept pace with increases in per capita disposable income, it has moved well beyond it. The average annual growth rate of per capita disposable income over the decade of the sixties was 5 percent per year. The average rate of increase in tuition and fees, however, was 7.5 percent over the same period.

Another problem for private institutions is the widening tuition gap between private and public institutions. The average rate of increase in tuition and fees for all institutions in the United States, Earl Cheit has noted, was 7.5 percent, and for public institutions, 5.8 percent. Each year the split becomes wider. Tuition rises in both private and tax-supported institutions but at different rates because tuition is the major source of income to which private institutions turn to meet escalating costs while tax-supported institutions have other primary sources of income.

---

[1] William G. Bowen, *The Economics of the Major Private Universities* (Berkeley, Calif.: Carnegie Commission on Higher Education, 1968), p. 21. Hans H. Jenny and G. Richard Wynn, *The Golden Years* (Wooster, Ohio, 1972), pp. 52–54.

With this growing divergence in tuition it is becoming increasingly difficult for higher education to go forward equally dependent upon both private and public institutions. It is rather like trying to walk two rails that diverge from one another at a slight angle. One cannot proceed very far before the gap between them becomes first awkward, then impossible. For many individual applicants, in fact, higher education has already ceased to be a dual system. This steadily widening divergence has left them with no real choice.

Gifts and Grants

In one sense a college appears to be more secure if it has multiple sources of income rather than a single source of income. A college is not unique in this respect. Communities dependent upon several small industries generally enjoy better economic health over the long run than communities like those along the River Clyde in Scotland, dependent upon shipbuilding, or those in our own Pacific Northwest, so largely dependent upon the aircraft industry. Mutual funds and conglomerate corporations reflect this same conviction about multiple sources of income.

With its eggs scattered in several baskets the college will not be driven off the landscape if one of its baskets breaks, for economic or other reasons. It need not be altogether at the mercy of disaffected donors, of a religious body, of the stock market, of state and federal legislators. If only one of these sources of support fails, the college will not be brought to its knees, *provided it has a financial cushion* either in the form of surplus funds or in the form of expenditures which it can immediately reduce while it simultaneously rebudgets and moves to develop other potential sources of income.

For the other side of this multiple-sources-of-income coin is that there are multiple donors to be cultivated and multiple threats to the college's economy. For the college's economy to function smoothly a large number of parts, both income and expenditure items, must work in harmony with each of the others. Institutions of higher learning typically build their programs to the limits of their incomes. If any source of income fails, the other income and expenditure parts are affected by its failure.

This is the implicit threat to private institutions as they turn to increased state and federal aid. To have students enrolled who are dependent upon the fiscal fortunes of the state, for example, is to leave the institution in which they are enrolled the residuary legatee of a moral obligation if the state defaults on its commitments. Moreover, a college begins to bend some features of its program to a source of income as a plant bends in the direction of light. If that source fails, the college will be caught in an awkward position until it can adjust. One contemporary illustration of this is the difficulty in which many universities have found themselves with a diminution of research funds from federal agencies but with a commitment to students and staff based upon the expectation that those funds would continue. The outline of another illustration may be taking shape in states with strong programs of state scholarship aid to students. Institutions in those states turn more and more to the cultivation of the local market even if the institution formerly drew students from the region or from the nation. If that state aid were to fail, the colleges could not immediately restore their out-of-state markets. Each source of income is a potential threat to the financial security of the college.

One of the major sources of income in private colleges and universities, recorded in the educational and general account as gifts and grants, is a multiple set of sources: corporations, foundations, churches, alumni, local constituencies, friends. Private institutions build each year's budget on the expectation of substantial support from these sources. Not many colleges have reached the stage where they can build next year's budget around this year's gifts. Next year's budget is built around next year's gifts. This leaves the delicate balance of the institution's financial situation subject to sudden shifts in the weight of opinion or fortune. If the economy experiences a downturn, as happened in 1970 and 1971, corporate giving goes down. If an unfavorable tax act is passed, as happened in 1969, philanthropic giving goes down. If student unrest angers alumni and other donors, as happened in 1970, alumni contributions go down. Since the money goes immediately from the hand of the donor into the mouth of the current budget, the effect of any of these shifts is immediate. The college is already operating with its commitments and fixed costs. If the money does not arrive, the college runs a deficit.

Strictly speaking, the gift and grant money reported in the current fund income and expenditures statement should be only that money actually expended in the year in which it is entered. The money recorded by the responding institutions in these data should, therefore, be those revenues actually applied to the current operations. If gifts and bequests are held for later application to the current fund or for transfer to plant, quasi-endowment, or loan funds, they should have been recorded elsewhere. Restricted gifts, similarly, should be reported in the operating account in any fiscal period only to the extent that they were actually expended during that period in accordance with the conditions of the gift.

It is not pellucidly clear that these accounting niceties were scrupulously observed in reporting these data. Even more important, we became aware during the editing process that the distinctions between restricted gifts and grants—those which the institution receives with terms and conditions attached—and unrestricted gifts and grants were not always observed. While the combined total probably accurately reflects total gift and grant income, the distinctions between restricted and unrestricted appear sometimes arbitrary. Comparisons between them should not be stretched too far. When restricted and unrestricted gifts and grants are added together, the national picture looks like this: increases (noncumulative) of 10.7 (1968 to 1969), 2.6 (1969 to 1970), and (anticipated) 6.4 percent (1970 to 1971).

However, restricted and unrestricted gifts and grants are quite different in their effect on the institution. Restricted gifts may have to be used for purposes that are not high on the institution's priority list. They may, in fact, provide money only for additional programs and may not release any institutional funds for programs the institution considers primary. Over the years covered by these data, unrestricted gifts and grants—the larger and, because of the greater flexibility they afford the institution, more welcome of the two kinds—increased 6.7 percent between 1968 and 1969, 8.6 percent between 1969 and 1970, and were expected to increase by 7.3 percent the following year. Restricted gifts and grants followed a much different pattern. They increased by 16.7 percent the first year, decreased 5.6 percent between 1969 and 1970, and were expected to increase again by 5 percent the year following.

Unrestricted gifts and grants play a much larger role in the economic life of small institutions than of large ones. In general, the larger the institution, the smaller the percentage of educational and general income derived from unrestricted gifts and grants. The Smallest institutions depend upon unrestricted gifts and grants for one-sixth of their educational and general income. In Largest institutions the fraction is one-twentieth. The same is not true with regard to restricted gifts and grants. They play a big role in the life of very small institutions; but they also play a big role in large institutions. In Smallest institutions the percentage of educational and general income derived from restricted gifts and grants is less than half the amount received from unrestricted gifts. In Largest institutions, however, restricted gifts constitute a larger percentage of income than unrestricted gifts. Because unrestricted gift and grant income is generally greater than restricted gift and grant income, the rule of thumb again applies when they are combined, namely, the larger the institution, the smaller the role played in educational and general income by gifts and grants.

If medical center and sponsored research revenues are withdrawn from educational and general income, however, that statement must be modified. While it remains substantially true with regard to unrestricted gifts and grants, it is not accurate for restricted gifts and grants or for both added together. In fact, restricted gifts alone are then actually a larger percentage of educational and general income for the group of institutions with the largest enrollments than for the group with the smallest.

While the rule of thumb with regard to size is that the larger the institution, the smaller the role played by income from gifts and grants, the same is not true with regard to the degree of complexness. In fact, although it is a scattered pattern, something close to the obverse is true. With medical center and sponsored research excluded, the institutions offering the highest degree derive a larger percentage of income from gifts and grants than those institutions offering only lower degrees. Nearly 20 percent of the educational and general income of doctoral degree granting institutions comes

Table 10. PERCENTAGE OF GENERAL INCOME DERIVED
FROM GIFTS AND GRANTS: 1969

	Including Sponsored Research and Medical Center Income		
	Unrestricted	Restricted	Together
Institutions by Enrollment Size			
Smallest	16.6	6.7	23.3
Small	12.0	3.9	15.9
Medium	8.8	3.2	12.0
Large	6.8	4.2	11.0
Largest	4.9	5.7	10.6
	Excluding Sponsored Research and Medical Center Income		
	Unrestricted	Restricted	Together
Smallest	16.8	6.8	23.6
Small	12.1	3.9	16.0
Medium	9.0	3.3	12.3
Large	7.8	4.8	12.6
Largest	8.0	9.3	17.3

from gifts and grants. For the groups of institutions offering only lower degrees, they account for 10 to 15 percent.

When these institutions are regrouped by budget levels with medical center and sponsored research revenues included, one can say with only one slight modification that the larger the budget, the smaller the percentage played by unrestricted gifts and grants in the educational and general income budget. The same is true when medical center and sponsored research revenues are excluded except for institutions with a budget of fifteen million or more. And, by either reckoning, this group derives a larger percentage of income from restricted gifts and grants than any other budget level group.

Institutions with educational and general budgets under fifteen million dollars are not much influenced by sponsored research—let alone medical center—revenues. When restricted and unrestricted gifts and grants are combined, regardless of whether sponsored research and medical center revenues are included or excluded, institutions with budgets under two million dollars receive about 16 percent of their income from gifts; those with budgets between two and four million receive less than 4 percent; and those with budgets between four and fifteen million receive between 9 and 12 percent. The substantial effect of both sponsored research and medical center revenues on institutions with budgets over fifteen million dollars alters the percentage received from gifts and grants from 11 percent (with the revenues included) to 20 percent (with the revenues excluded).

Church Support

One of the especially interesting sources of educational and general revenue on which we have specific data from these institutions is the support offered by some religious body. Most of this would be subsumed under gifts and grants except that for most Roman Catholic related institutions and some Lutheran ones, the larger part of this support may be subsumed under the discrete category of contributed services.

The best way to define church relationship and the best ways to live with it have long been matters of ecclesiastical and academic debate for church-related colleges and their supporting denominational bodies. The questions have grown sharper in recent years for a variety of reasons. To meet the rigidities of some state constitutions, institutions that until recently proudly affirmed a church relationship are now claiming independent status. In some instances, either affirmation could be made with little adjustment in the structure of the institution itself, such are the vagaries of definitions of church relationship.

For our purposes, however, church relationship was defined in financial terms: by church support. Hence, if an institution claimed to be independent but received church support, we overruled the self-designation and identified the institution with its denominational group if we knew its parentage. Some sixteen colleges escaped this effort for additional identification and thus present us with the apparent anomaly of being "independent" colleges with church support.

In addition to financial support that comes from some ecclesiastical body called "church," there is a very important financial contribution made by other religious bodies which is contributed services. These contributions by religious orders—typically, but not exclusively Roman Catholic—are not church support in a narrow sense but they are a very important kind of contribution so closely akin to church support as to deserve to be treated with it.

There are also, of course, gifts from individual donors that spring from the donor's identification of the college or university as a church-related institution or one, at least, in which the donor's religiously related intent can be given expression. However, this category of income would be very difficult to define and would not carry us very far in this analysis. Even tax-supported institutions are often beneficiaries of such giving.

Previous analyses of the contributions of church bodies to their related colleges have been based upon information supplied by the denominations and reckoned in terms of total dollars, dollars per institution, and dollars per capita member of the denomination.

What we provide here is an analysis based upon data supplied by the colleges themselves, which can be seen in terms of total dollars, dollars per institution, dollars per full time equivalent student, and, most meaningful from the college's standpoint, a comparison of church support in terms of percentage of the college or university's current fund income and current fund expenditures. Since these data are for a single year (1969), one cannot know how representative this year was nor what trends may have been developing; and for some denominational groups we are reporting on a rather small population relying, in some instances, on a limited sample. Nevertheless, the reader will find the comparisons interesting.

Seventh Day Adventists support their colleges more handsomely than any other denominational body, providing over a million dollars a year, on the average, to each of their institutions. Not surprisingly, theirs is also the largest contribution in terms of support as a percentage of current fund expenditure. It is nearly 12 percent of the budget.

The second largest supporter in terms of average dollars per institution is the Southern Baptist denomination which supplies its institutions an average $282,000 per year. On the basis of support as a percentage of budget, second place belongs to the Church of the Nazarene which provides its colleges nearly 10 percent of their current fund budgets.

As the following table indicates, five denominations average over $200,000 per year in support to their colleges and eight denominations provide over 5 percent of the current operating fund budgets of the colleges related to them.

Table 11. CHURCH SUPPORT BY DENOMINATION: PER AVERAGE INSTITUTION: 1969

Ranking by Dollars Provided (in thousands)		Ranking in Terms of Church Support as a Percentage of Current Fund Expenditures[a]	
			Percent
$1179	Seventh Day Adventist	Seventh Day Adventist	11.8
282	Southern Baptist	Church of the Nazarene	9.9
262	Lutheran Church in America	Southern Baptist	7.6
		Roman Catholic	5.9
253	Roman Catholic (with contributed services)	Lutheran Church in America	5.9
238	Church of the Nazarene	Reformed Church in	
172	Reformed Church in America	America	5.7
		Other	5.6
164	American Lutheran Church	Mennonite	5.0
		Presbyterian, U.S.	3.8
145	Other	American Lutheran	
127	Presbyterian, U.S.	Church	3.3
107	Disciples of Christ	Church of the Brethren	2.9
106	Methodist	Disciples of Christ	2.8
97	Mennonite	American Baptist	
94	Church of the Brethren	Convention	2.6
84	American Baptist Convention	Methodist	2.2
		United Presbyterian,	
61	United Presbyterian, U.S.A.	U.S.A.	2.0
		United Church of Christ	1.9
55	United Church of Christ		

[a] The spread between groups is great enough so that with two minor exceptions the same order of ranking prevails whether the measure is current fund income or current fund expenditure.

It will come as no surprise to the colleges that, although all colleges related to a given denomination may lay claim to that relationship equal to any other college so related, when it comes to support from the denomination, some are more equal than others. Colleges related to the Seventh Day Adventist group average over a million dollars a year. One of them, however, reports receiving only $282,000 while one of them reports receiving nearly four million dollars. The median—as distinct from the average—Seventh Day Adventist institution received $385,000.

The average annual support figure of $282,000 for colleges related to the Southern Baptist Church is a more accurate reflection of their typical church support than is true for Seventh Day Adventist colleges. Church support for Southern Baptist institutions ranges from as little as $40,000 to as much as $630,000 but their median institution received $242,000. One quarter of these colleges received $189,000 or less; one quarter received $376,000 or more.

Nowhere is the arithmetical deception of the average clearer than in the case of institutions related to the Roman Catholic Church. In response to our specific inquiry on church support, only twenty-one of these colleges, 13 percent of the Roman Catholic colleges in our sample, reported receiving any. The church support they did receive varied from a low of two-thousand dollars to a high of nearly 3.4 million dollars with a median level of support, among the twenty-one, of $86,000. Church support is interpreted by these respondents as being that kind of aid which passes directly from the ecclesiastical structure by way of some member of the hierarchy, typically, the bishop of the diocese in which the college is located.

That which gives most of the Roman Catholic colleges their sense of religious identity, however, is the Catholic religious order which brought them into being and which has sustained them through the services (especially teaching services) which members of that order give to the college. The contributed services of the order offer a subsidy to the college's operation as a sort of living endowment that often makes the difference between survival and death. When we add the value of the contributed services received by these colleges to the support received from the ecclesiastical church structure, we gain a better measurement of the dimensions of support received from religious bodies and how this compares with the support received by colleges related to other religious bodies.

Seventeen of the Roman Catholic colleges report no support

from the church and no income from contributed services. It may be that their support from the order is to be found in the unrestricted or restricted gifts received by the college. Of late, some colleges and their sustaining religious orders have established a relationship whereby the college pays each teaching member of the order a salary commensurate with equally qualified lay members of the faculty, and then the order returns those salaries as a gift to the college. If we include these seventeen colleges with the others, the average amount of church support and contributed services is $253,000. The median institution receives $222,000. If we were to subtract these colleges from the total, the average for the remaining 142 colleges and universities would be $283,000 and the median would be $241,000.

The highs, lows, and median figures on institutional support for colleges reporting receiving support from religious bodies are set forth in Table 12 arranged in order of median levels.

When analyzed on a per student basis there are no big surprises. The Seventh Day Adventist group heads the list on an institutional basis; it also heads the list on a per student basis. Its median institution receives $385,000; its median institution in terms of support per full-time equivalent student receives $358 for each full-time or full-time equivalent student. The median Roman Catholic institution in terms of support per student is in second place with $275 of support and the Southern Baptists are third with $217.

In terms of support from a religious body on a per student basis an institution is better off if it is small; but not necessarily better off if it is less complex. The difference by size is so marked that it almost appears as if a supporting religious body thinks in terms of support for an institution (or group of institutions); not how many students attend. This may be a holdover from the days when the colleges themselves thought of revenues and expenditures less in terms of the individual student than in terms of the institution as a whole, almost as though the actual number of students was of little financial consequence.

At any rate, the median institution of those in the Smallest group receiving support from a religious body receives $465 per student. The median institution in the Small group receives $181. In the Medium group the figure is ninety-four dollars. It is ninety

Table 12. SUPPORT RECEIVED FROM RELIGIOUS BODIES:
BY DENOMINATION AND ON PER-STUDENT BASIS: 1969

Denominational Group	Median	Low	High
Institutional Basis			
(in thousands of dollars)			
Seventh Day Adventist	$385	$282	$3894
Southern Baptist	242	40	630
Roman Catholic	241	5	3382
Lutheran Church in America	183	47	695
Church of the Nazarene	226	164	335
Reformed Church in America	176	140	200
American Lutheran Church	164	117	259
Independent	91	2	426
Disciples of Christ	88	9	264
Mennonite	85	32	200
Methodist	85	20	474
Presbyterian, U.S.	84	9	372
Church of the Brethren	80	41	222
United Presbyterian, U.S.A.	52	27	250
United Church of Christ	47	10	152
Other	47	12	900
American Baptist Convention	44	10	383
Full-Time Equivalent			
Student Basis			
Seventh Day Adventist	358	282	1369
Roman Catholic	275	4	3714
Southern Baptist	217	29	532
Church of the Nazarene	200	119	415
Lutheran Church in America	172	34	950
Reformed Church in America	145	103	193
Mennonite	141	56	206
Presbyterian, U.S.	136	1	389
American Lutheran Church	85	79	142
Independent	80	1	1152
Methodist	74	9	385
Disciples of Christ	67	11	190
Other	55	10	258
Church of the Brethren	54	23	452
United Presbyterian, U.S.A.	51	14	216
American Baptist Convention	50	8	394
United Church of Christ	54	14	219

dollars in the Large group and forty-seven dollars in the Largest group.

The median institution among Bachelors institutions receives $131 per student. For the Limited Doctors group of institutions related to some religious body the median support figure is two dollars above this figure; for the Masters institutions it is two dollars less. It is ninety-nine dollars for Limited Masters institutions, and fifty-five dollars for Doctors institutions.

There is just enough difference regionally to make one or two observations worth reporting. Five geographic regions are very much like one another in terms of the dollar support received by the median religiously related institution on a per student basis. They fall within a nine dollar spread. They are the South Atlantic ($113), Pacific ($115), East North Central ($119), Mountain ($121), and West North Central ($122). Out of this common group falls the Middle Atlantic ($161), West South Central ($169), East South Central ($192), and New England ($293).

Endowment

Baseball players dream of pitching no hit games. Teenagers dream of being fantastically attractive to the opposite sex. Colleges dream of having an endowment like Harvard's. (Harvard dreams of having more.) The economic security and political independence seemingly provided by substantial endowment make it a unique income source.

Its strength as an economic defender may be overrated. In 1969 institutions running deficits of $600,000 or more received 12.6 percent of their educational and general income—minus sponsored research and medical center income—from endowment. Institutions running surpluses of $600,000 or more received only 4.6 percent.

The chief complaint against endowment, however, is that there is not much of it and not enough to keep pace with rising costs of higher education. The role played by endowment is diminishing. In 1969 the total educational and general expenditure budget for private colleges and universities increased 12.4 percent. Educational and general income from endowment increased only 8.5 percent. Endowment income increased the following year by

7.5 percent which very nearly kept pace with the educational and general expenditure increase of 7.9 percent; but the following year the anticipated increases were 5.5 percent for endowment income and 7.8 percent for educational and general expenditures.

Ninety-two percent of our responding institutions had a book value to report on endowment. The average was seven and a half million dollars ($7,508,000). Unfortunately, only 84 percent were able to report on the more significant aspect of endowments, their market value. The average was $9,636,000. In addition, 42 percent reported a market value for funds functioning as endowment at an average of better than three and a half million dollars ($3,754,000). The study also sought to find out what the market value was of that part of the total endowment (exclusive of funds functioning as endowment) which is unrestricted endowment. Sixty-one percent of the institutions responded by indicating an average market value in unrestricted endowment of $4,280,000. If each aspect of this question had been fully understood and answered by the same number of institutions in each case, we could say that the mean private institution has an endowment with a market value of 9.6 million dollars of which 44 percent, or 4.3 million dollars, is unrestricted, and has, in addition, 3.8 million in funds functioning as endowment. The unevenness of reporting and the apparent misunderstanding of the terms requires, however, that a statement as general as this one about the endowment of the mean institution be treated as a rough approximation.

The median figures reveal a much more modest endowment dowry than the mean figures suggest. Of reporting colleges and universities, the median private institution had a market value on true endowment (excluding funds functioning as endowment) of just under two million dollars ($1,955,000). The median institution among those reporting the market value of funds functioning as endowment reported $720,000. The median institution among those reporting market value on both true endowment and on funds functioning as endowment had a combined endowment figure of $3,536,000. One-fourth of those reporting a combined figure had an endowment with a market value in 1969 of 1¼ million dollars, or less, while another one fourth had a combined endowment of 18.5 million dollars or more.

A decile distribution of endowment funds is shown in the table below. This table makes clear that a large number of private institutions possess an endowment scarcely worthy of the name. For every institution with twenty-one million dollars or more in true endowment funds there are more than three with less than one million.

Table 13. DECILE DISTRIBUTION OF THE TRUE ENDOWMENT AND
OF FUNDS FUNCTIONING AS ENDOWMENT OF ALL PRIVATE
COLLEGES AND UNIVERSITIES:
(market value in millions of dollars) : 1969

Deciles	True Endowment (84% reporting)	Funds Functioning as Endowment (42% reporting)
1st decile	less than 0.2	less than .05
2nd decile	0.2 to 0.5	0.05 to 0.1
3rd decile	0.5 to 0.8	0.1 to 0.3
4th decile	0.8 to 1.3	0.3 to 0.4
5th decile	1.3 to 2.0	0.4 to 0.7
6th decile	2.0 to 3.1	0.7 to 1.1
7th decile	3.1 to 5.0	1.1 to 1.8
8th decile	5.0 to 9.6	1.8 to 3.0
9th decile	9.6 to 21.4	3.0 to 6.2
10th decile	more than 21.4	more than 6.2

Except for the few reporting institutions related to the Episcopal Church, those which are independent of church relationship have a larger endowment than any of those groups of institutions bearing a denominational affiliation. The following Table includes only denominations with at least three institutions reporting a market value for true endowment.

Regionally, the average institution in New England has an endowment larger than the average institution in any other region. The median New England institution has a true endowment of $10,202,000. The next largest, running poor seconds, are the median institutions in the West South Central and South Atlantic regions with true endowments slightly over $2,500,000. In the Mountain, West North Central, and Mid-Atlantic regions, the median institution is below the national median of $1,955,000. The

Table 14. MARKET VALUE OF TRUE ENDOWMENT: BY AVERAGE (MEAN) AND MEDIAN DENOMINATIONAL INSTITUTION: 1969

	Mean	Median
	(in millions)	
Independent	$21.7	$ 6.0
Episcopal	16.8	21.9
Southern Baptist	10.0	2.8
Methodist	7.4	3.4
Disciples of Christ	6.0	1.2
United Presbyterian, U.S.A.	5.0	2.5
American Baptist Convention	4.4	1.2
Presbyterian, U.S.	3.8	2.5
Lutheran Church in America	3.0	2.0
United Church of Christ	3.0	2.1
Quaker	1.7	1.5
American Lutheran Church	1.6	1.3
Roman Catholic	1.5	0.5
Reformed Church in America	1.5	1.5
Other	1.4	0.9
Church of the Brethren	1.1	1.1
Seventh Day Adventist	0.8	1.5
Mennonite	0.8	0.8

dollar distance between median institutions in the various regions reporting funds functioning as endowment is narrow. In the East South Central and West North Central regions the figure is below half a million dollars. In the West South Central, East North Central, and South Atlantic regions it is between one-half and one million dollars. The figure is between one and 1½ million in the remaining regions, except for New England where the figure is $1,746,000.

On the average, the larger the institution and the more complex its program (as judged by degree level) the larger the size of the endowment held by the institution. This fact probably occasions little surprise. There are well endowed institutions that are both small and not complex, even as there are others that are large and complex but poorly endowed. But typically, endowment exists in a reciprocal relationship with size and complexity. The institution has grown both bigger and more complex in response to its endowment and this growth in turn has tended to enhance the growth of its endowment.

The wide disparity between mean and median figures—for all enrollment and degree level groups except Limited Doctor's—is simple evidence that a few institutions in each group have a much larger endowment than the others. This raises the mean. The median figure is more indicative of the thinness of the padding in the endowment cushion for the institutions in that group.

Table 15. MARKET VALUE OF TRUE ENDOWMENT AND OF FUNDS FUNCTIONING AS ENDOWMENT FOR THE MEAN AND MEDIAN REPORTING INSTITUTIONS: (in millions): 1969

	True Endowment[a]		Funds Functioning as Endowment[a]	
	Mean	Median	Mean	Median
Geographic Regions				
Nation	$ 9.6	$ 2.0	$ 3.7	$ .7
Pacific	5.6	2.3	1.9	1.2
Mountain	2.5	0.8	1.2	1.5
West South Central	7.0	2.6	3.3	.8
East South Central	8.5	2.3	3.8	.3
West North Central	4.9	1.5	1.1	.3
East North Central	4.7	2.0	2.3	.7
South Atlantic	10.3	2.6	5.2	.8
Mid-Atlantic	10.3	1.4	4.3	1.1
New England	35.4	10.2	8.4	1.7
Enrollment Groups				
Smallest	1.2	.4	.5	.1
Small	3.3	1.3	.8	.3
Medium	6.7	2.4	2.1	.7
Large	9.0	2.9	1.3	.8
Largest	38.0	6.4	11.4	2.8
Degree Levels				
Bachelor's	3.6	1.3	1.1	.3
Limited Master's	6.3	1.7	1.8	.8
Master's	7.4	2.9	2.3	.9
Limited Doctor's	14.6	10.7	4.8	3.6
Doctor's	62.0	24.5	20.0	9.6

[a] These amounts should not be added because only approximately one half as many institutions report a figure for funds functioning as endowment as report true endowment.

When endowment is figured on a full-time equivalent student basis, however, a much modified order prevails. Endowment does not routinely increase as the institution increases in size and complexity. Small institutions have a larger true endowment per student at the median than all other enrollment groups. These true endowment figures, together with per student figures for those institutions reporting market values for funds functioning as endowment, are found in Table 16 for the enrollment groups:

Table 16.   ENDOWMENT VALUE PER FULL-TIME EQUIVALENT STUDENT: 1969

	True Endowment	Funds Functioning as Endowment
Enrollment Groups		
Smallest	$1240	$ 280
Small	1950	410
Median	1750	520
Large	1160	410
Largest	680	450
Degree Levels		
Bachelor's	1620	360
Limited Master's	1110	620
Master's	1000	440
Limited Doctor's	2040	680
Doctor's	5400	2050

Doctoral degree granting institutions have the largest endowment per student of any of the degree level groups, but Masters institutions, have the smallest true endowment per student.

Sources of Student Aid

Responding institutions were asked the sources of money for the direct student aid they provided during the two most recently completed fiscal years (1968 and 1969) and to estimate on 1970. These are not data that require the end of the fiscal year for accurate reporting and therefore need not be considered projected data in the same sense in which other income and expenditure data must be. In addition, we asked that our respondents project data for 1971 and 1972.

Sources of student aid, including scholarships, grants, prizes, and loans, were broken down into general institutional operating funds, endowment or funds functioning as endowment, private funds, and federal and state funds.

Based on their responses, institutions fell into three categories: (A.) those whose total student aid expenditures from four sources equalled the amount for student aid previously reported in the data under current fund expenditures; (B.) those whose total student aid from these four sources did not equal the amount listed under current fund expenditures, presumably because they included NDEA and other loan money when responding to this question but did not include such funds in their current fund accounts; (C.) the residue of responses that fell into neither of these categories. The data for this group are neither internally consistent nor consistent with current fund data. Reluctantly concluding that—even allowing for the notorious caprice with which economic answers allegedly change—their responses were not answers to our questions, we put group C in fiscal quarantine in order not to contaminate the remaining data. It is necessary to report this division because our useable response rate necessarily suffers in regard to these data. Except for some geographic variation, the institutions in each category do not differ greatly from one another on the basis of demographic data.

Approximately 47 percent of our respondents fell into category A, 31 percent into category B, and 23 percent into category C. About category C we have nothing further to say. Institutions in category A (whose student aid data probably does not include federal loan money) provided the following information.

Forty percent of the money they expended on direct student aid came from general operating funds in 1968; 11 percent came from endowment or funds functioning as endowment; 12 percent from private funds; and the remaining 36 percent from federal and state funds.

Ninety-five percent of those institutions reported putting money from general operating funds into direct student aid. Eighty-five percent indicated that federal and state funds were included in their student aid expenditure. Seventy-six percent reported the use of endowment or funds functioning as endowment, and an identical percentage reported the use of private funds. Private funds are nongovernmental monies from sources external to the institution and intended for use in the current year. An example would be a scholarship awarded by a business corporation.

The trends revealed by the institutions in group A are not particularly encouraging. For one thing, these institutions projected a progressive rise in the percentage of support for direct student aid coming from the institution's general operating funds. For the five years covered by these data the percentage increases as follows: 40, 40, 43, 45, and 46 percent. The percentage expected to come from endowment stays virtually constant. The percentage expected from private funds falls off 2 percent while the percentage expected from federal and state funds, after an initial rise, falls away by 6 percentage points: 36, 37, 35, 33, 31 percent.

The need to provide from their own funds support for students previously covered by funds from the federal government is a problem of growing magnitude for some institutions. The number of institutions reporting that they were replacing with their own funds grant and loan money formerly supplied by the federal government, although small, showed a steady increase over a four year period. In 1966 thirteen institutions reported that they were providing loan money to students out of institutional funds that the federal government had been providing. In 1970, five times as many institutions so reported. Similarly, in 1965 there were twenty-two institutions that said they were providing grants out of institutional funds to students who formerly received support from the federal government. In 1970, four times as many institutions so reported. The dollars involved went from $866,000 in grant and loan money in 1966 to over ten times that amount in 1970.

Money available for student aid from all sources fell off abruptly after a sharp initial rise. On a per-reporting-institution basis, total student aid rose 17.5 percent in 1969 over 1968, 9.8 percent in 1970 and was expected to rise by only 1.6 percent in 1972.

Because expenditures continued to rise faster than income for student aid, the deficit in the account also rose faster. Total income for student aid for all private institutions showed a cumulative increase from 1968 to 1971 of 28 percent, while expenditures grew 38 percent, causing the deficit in this account to increase 50 percent. As this gap widens it must be covered by institutional funds.

For many private institutions, this deficit in the student aid account is equal to the total deficit in the whole current fund account.

Grouping the institutions into various degree level categories, it is interesting to note that the Limited Master's group of institutions derives the largest percentage (61 percent) of student aid from institutional funds—49 percent from current operating funds and 12 percent from endowment—and the lowest percentage (29 percent) from federal and state funds. The Limited Doctor's group derives the lowest percentage (44 percent) from institutional funds —37 percent from current funds and 7 percent from endowment— and the highest percentage (47 percent) from federal and state funds. Bachelor's, Master's, and Doctor's institutions percentages closely approximate the collective averages noted earlier.

When institutions are grouped by size of enrollment, the percentage of student aid derived from general institutional operating funds is nearly the same in all five groups (from 41 to 45 percent) as also is the percentage derived from private sources (from 10 to 13 percent). The discrepancy is larger between the Smallest group and the Medium group; the percentage of aid derived from endowment is 4 percent for the former and 15 percent for the latter, and the percentage derived from federal and state funds is 41 percent for the Smallest and 28 percent for the Medium. The remaining percentages closely approximate the collective figures.

Examined by regions, the most striking differences lie in the percentages of institutions that fell in group A. Sixty percent of the colleges and universities in the New England region reported on sources of student aid in a way that agreed with the current fund account, but only 16 percent of those in the West South Central region did. Institutions in the West North Central region were dependent upon their institutional operating funds for 54 percent of the student aid they provided in 1970, while institutions in the Pacific region were dependent upon this source for only 36 percent. Institutions in the remaining regions fell close to the national average of 43 percent.

Endowment, and funds functioning as endowment, constituted 18 percent of the student aid provided by institutions in the New England region but only 7 percent in the East and West North Central regions. Private sources accounted for 15 percent of the student aid offered by institutions in the East North Central region and 10 percent of the aid offered by institutions in the Mid-Atlantic region. Federal and state funds constituted 39 percent of the student aid offered by institutions in the East North Central region and 23 percent of the aid offered by institutions in the New England region.

Auxiliary Enterprises

One of the sources of current fund income—according to the ways most of our respondents keep their books—is auxiliary enterprises. Some institutions, the Department of Housing and Urban Development will tell you, have made a substantial amount of money (over and above debt service payments) on their residence halls. These institutions may be laboring under the same delusion that was evident in one company that kept its books on the basis of location. As a result, the sales office in New York—where the income was—was doing beautifully; but they were losing their shirts manufacturing their product in St. Louis. If space taken by the bookstore or the land used by a residence hall is not charged as rent, if a portion of the heating plant is not allocated to these activities, if administrative costs are not assigned to them, then auxiliary enterprises frequently show a surplus of income over expenditure which helps compensate for the deficit in the student aid account.

According to the data supplied for the four years 1968 through 1971, the average institution in every enrollment group except the Largest was showing a profit in its operation of auxiliary enterprises, and even the Largest group expected to be close to the break–even point by the end of 1971. By degree levels, the average institution in each group is making money on auxiliary enterprises except for the Doctors group, and they hoped to be losing in 1971 only 40 percent of what they were losing in 1969.

Future Income Planning

The cynic who observes that the source of higher education's financial plight lies with its income, not with its expenditures, has an essential element of truth on his side. During the decade of the sixties the colleges took what they could get—and spent it. Higher education's share of the country's gross national product grew from 1 percent in 1960 to 2.5 percent in 1970. An expansive economy, rapid enrollment growth, a supportive and beneficent society, flowed together to send a mighty stream of financial support into the nation's colleges and universities.

No one seems to have perceived the need for careful planning and the setting of priorities. In a dynamic and growing institution one simply adds the next good thing to do. One has little inclination either to challenge existing programs or to consider the long-range implications of new ones. Growth carried the illusion of permanency, and beguiled the normally cautious campus administrator from serious thought that the future might not bring continued growth, might be static, or might even bring a decline. Confronted by ever increasing demands, colleges and universities responded in a forceful, positive manner. In so doing they helped set the stage for their financial problems. When the black ink of income began to clot, the red ink of expenditure continued to flow and the colleges were caught overextended and largely unprepared.

Private institutions of higher learning do not want to believe that their rate of income growth may remain at a low level for a long time, or that they can permanently solve their financial problems by not returning to their former high rate of income growth. Thus, the Priorities Committee at Princeton University, in 1971, after projecting relatively modest income growth rates for the next two or three years stated that it remained convinced that the only satisfactory long-term solution lay in a return to the high income growth rate it had previously enjoyed. The signs are against this happening soon.

The single largest source of increased income for most private institutions is tuition. Yet that source of increased income is beginning to dry up. When, early in 1973, President Terry Sanford of Duke University noted that private colleges are about to be priced out of the market, he was talking in a total sense. The plain fact is that for some institutions and for many students the private sector has already been priced out of the market. Studies in one state after the other show that private institutions are able to compete successfully with public institutions under a tuition price differential until that difference becomes too great. Each increase in the differential is accompanied by a companion decrease in the number of students able and willing to pay it. The median resident tuition increase in state colleges and universities in fiscal 1973 was a modest twenty-three dollars while private college tuitions continued to escalate. In recent years the differential has increased at the rate of one-hundred and fifty dollars per year, but the gap between the two may be widening even faster. This year the differential approaches two-thousand dollars. The difference between the numbers of students able to pay an additional six-hundred and fifty dollars—as they did in 1964—and those able to pay an additional two-thousand dollars—as they must today—is marked and measurable.

Although one obviously would not want to set public tuitions (uncoupled with other aid) so high that both public and private higher education are placed beyond the reach of many students, some rise in public tuitions appears desirable and inevitable. A happier answer is to provide greater financial aid to students attending private institutions so they can again become financially competitive in the eyes of the students.

At the same time, it is clearly evident to many observers that a greater fraction of the rising cost of higher education will have to be shifted to the recipient of that education, not simply because he is a primary beneficiary but because he will be able to pay if, in addition to grant programs, he is aided by improved loan programs. The debate about the degrees of individual and social benefit derived from higher education should not obscure this fundamental point. The individual should not be deprived of the opportunity to offer the social benefit of his education as his gift to his society.

This argument suggests, to this writer, that some kind of federally sponsored income-contingency loan plan should be created. Such a plan, under which a student could borrow money toward the total cost of his education while being insured against failure, would improve the distribution and uniformity of borrowing opportunities. It would maximize the freedom of the student, reduce the opportunity for governmental interference in the affairs of the institution, while weaving its way around church and state issues with less torture than other devices for channeling federal money into public and private higher education. We have become a credit nation. Creating the capital good of higher education is, as Roger Bolton noted, an act of investment.[2] Since "it is something which pays off its cost over a very long period," it seems reasonable to exercise credit to obtain it and to pay for it over an equally long period. What higher education needs is programs that will help make income available on a long–range basis rather than on a one–shot or short–range basis. A student loan bank fits into that kind of need.

Another plan which deserves careful consideration, for the same reason, is put forward by Frederic Patterson of the Moton Memorial Foundation. The intent of Patterson's plan is to secure endowment funds for colleges and universities which will provide them with long-range income and stability. In this plan the federal government would provide subsidized loan funds according to a formula by which colleges must secure matching endowment funds from alumni or other donors. The combined amount would be invested, and annual payments derived from the investment return would be made to the government to repay principal and interest. At the end of the loan period the loan would be repaid, and the institution would be left with its endowment. This plan also has the merit of entailing a minimum of entanglement between the government and the college.

Specific proposals apart, what must be found are new, substantial, and long-range sources of income. Traditional sources appear insufficiently elastic to keep stretching to meet increasing costs. Voluntary support for private institutions was up only 1.9 percent in 1970–71 over the previous year, and most of that gain was due to increased support in professional and specialized schools. Major private universities actually experienced a 1.8 percent decline. Tuition—without some modification in the tuition differential coupled with additional grant and loan money to students—is showing the limits of its elasticity. Endowment—apart from a plan to support some dramatic development—is not keeping pace with costs. The contributed services provided some institutions by teaching members of a religious order is diminishing. Contributed services

[2] Roger E. Bolton, *The Public Financing of Higher Education* (Washington, D.C.: Brookings Institution, 1967).

are now declining and are destined to decline still further, especially in the small institutions. Not only has enlistment in the religious orders fallen off, but the order that formerly returned to the college as a gift the salaries earned by its members working in the college finds that it cannot be as generous as formerly. The order must provide for the retirement of its older members as well as for the education of its young religious. In short, like the churches, the religious orders find other and competing demands on the same set of resources at the very moment when those resources are declining.

Private institutions can be expected to turn to themselves to relieve the continuing imbalance between income and expenditure. This will require more efficient management, an aggressive search for private funds, and some diminished expectations of program; but they must have additional support at the state and federal levels if they are to remain viable.

IV

Where Does the
Money Go?

"Where does the money come from?", with its complexities of fluctuating interdependencies among income sources, is a large and important question. A bigger question for private colleges and universities is not where does the money come from, but, where does it go, and why so fast? As one business manager said perplexedly, "The trouble is not with my budget. That works out well enough. The trouble is that when I get to the end of my budget I still have a lot of calendar left." Whether there are too many days for the dollar or too few dollars for the days, the result is that in a great many institutions, more has been going out than coming in.

The smallest educational and general budget reported to us for 1969 was $370,000. This is, obviously, a very small institution; yet even this budget hints at the magnitude of the enterprise that is higher education. The median educational and general budget for each of the degree level groups was:

Bachelor's	$ 1,500,000
Limited Master's	2,800,000
Master's	3,700,000
Limited Doctor's	9,400,000
Doctor's	22,000,000

The median educational and general budget for each of the enrollment groups was:

Smallest	$ 700,000
Small	1,300,000
Medium	2,400,000
Large	4,200,000
Largest	16,000,000

That is a lot of courses in political science, books in the library, and coal for the furnace.

In an average expenditure budget, 50.4 percent goes for instruction and departmental research. General administration, student services, staff benefits, and general institutional expenses account for exactly half that amount, 25.2 percent. The operation and maintenance of the physical plant, at 12.0 percent, accounts for approximately half of the remainder, while libraries account for 5.3 percent, and all other expenses are responsible for 7.1 percent.

When medical center and sponsored research expenditures are included, the effect is to depress the percentages for other items. The way these two presentations of percentages compare with one another is set forth visually in Figure 4.

As institutions increase in size, they spend a larger percentage of their educational and general dollar on instruction and departmental research, and a smaller percentage on the operation and maintenance of the physical plant. Similarly, the smaller the institution the higher the proportion of the budget spent on general institutional expenses. Libraries, however, capture the 5 percent (in all budgets from which sponsored research and medical center expenses have been excluded) handed down from one generation of librarians to the next as a proper amount to spend on such things. These percentages are set forth in Table 17.

When private colleges are arranged in degree level groupings and examined for their educational and general expenditures, the

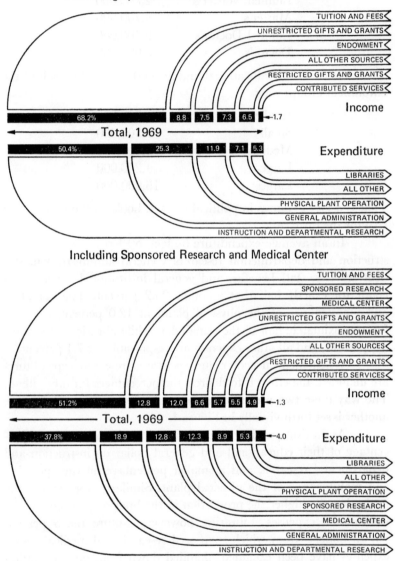

FIGURE 4. Income and expenditure distribution, educational and general account, all private colleges and universities, 1969.

data suggest that, in general, the more complex an institution in terms of degree level, the higher the percentage spent on instruction and departmental research. Both operation and maintenance of physical plant and general administration, student services, staff benefits, and general institutional expenses are a smaller percentage of the budget in the more complex institution. The shift in percentages for operation and maintenance of physical plant is very gentle. Size is a more important factor. The spread of percentages for general institutional expenses, however, is quite marked between each of the degree levels. Expenditures for libraries are fairly constant while expenditures for "all other" suggest more the vagaries of accounting systems than any intrinsic association with the degree level of the institution. These percentages are also in Table 17.

Faculty Compensation

Faculty compensation (salary and benefits) takes a big chunk out of the institutional budget. Together with departmental research and other items in the instruction budget, it is the largest single educational and general expenditure, consuming over 50 percent of the educational and general expenditure budget of all private colleges and universities (sponsored research and medical center expenditures excluded). We knew, from detailed educational and general budget data, what instruction and departmental research cost for 1968, 1969, and for the two following years on projected data. We enquired further about faculty compensation by professor, associate professor, and assistant professor, covering a five-year period: 1966 through 1970. By including data only from institutions that could supply information in all fifteen data categories we reduced the sample to 390 institutions. Average salaries were extracted from the median institution.

There were some marked geographical differences in the increase in the compensation of professors over the five-year period covered by our data. In the New England region the cumulative increase was only 26 percent while it was as high as 57 percent in the West South Central region. In dollar terms, however, the New England professor was making more at the start of the five-year period ($14,410) than his West South Central counterpart was

Table 17. Expenditure Distribution General and Educational Account: 1969

ENROLLMENT GROUPS

	Excluding Sponsored Research and Medical Center Expenses					Including Sponsored Research and Medical Center Expenses				
	Smallest	Small	Medium	Large	Largest	Smallest	Small	Medium	Large	Largest
Instruction and Departmental Research	43.3	45.4	47.9	48.6	53.7	42.9	44.9	47.0	42.3	32.7
Libraries	5.5	5.5	5.2	5.0	5.4	5.4	5.4	5.1	4.4	3.3
Operation and Maintenance of Physical Plant	16.0	12.9	12.4	12.0	11.3	15.8	12.8	12.2	10.4	6.9
General Administration, Student Services, Staff Benefits, General Institutional Expenses	30.9	30.8	28.8	27.0	21.4	30.6	30.5	28.3	23.5	13.0
Sponsored Research						1.0	1.0	1.8	5.0	19.1
Medical Center						0.0	0.0	0.0	8.0	20.0
All Other	4.3	5.4	5.7	7.4	8.2	4.3	5.4	5.6	6.4	5.0
Total	100.0	100.0	100.0	100.0	100.0	100.0	100.0	100.0	100.0	100.0

DEGREE LEVEL

	Bachelors	Limited Masters	Masters	Limited Doctors	Doctors	Bachelors	Limited Masters	Masters	Limited Doctors	Doctors
Instruction and Departmental Research	46.7	47.5	51.8	54.2	53.2	46.3	46.3	47.2	40.2	29.9
Libraries	5.3	5.0	5.0	5.1	5.5	5.2	4.9	4.6	3.8	3.1
Operation and Maintenance of Physical Plant	12.7	12.0	11.9	11.7	11.4	12.6	11.7	10.8	8.7	6.4
General Administration, Student Services, Staff Benefits, General Institutional Expenses	30.1	27.1	26.7	22.9	21.0	29.9	26.4	24.3	17.0	11.8
Sponsored Research						0.8	1.9	8.9	8.1	21.2
Medical Center						0.0	0.6	0.0	17.7	22.6
All Other	5.2	8.4	4.6	6.1	8.9	5.2	8.2	4.2	4.5	5.0
Total	100.0	100.0	100.0	100.0	100.0	100.0	100.0	100.0	100.0	100.0

making at the end of the period ($12,620); the New England pro-
fessor's edge was reduced from 79 percent to 44 percent. It is no
surprise that such differences exist. What is of special interest is
the range of those differences and the changes that are taking place
between them.

After the New England professor, the second most highly
compensated professor teaches in the Mid-Atlantic region. His compensation in 1970 was just under $17,000. Third was the professor
on the opposite coast and fourth was the professor in the East North
Central region. The dollar figures and their relation to cumulative
percentage increases for these regions and the other five regions are
set forth in Table 18.

Table 18. AVERAGE PROFESSORIAL COMPENSATION IN 1966 AND
1970 WITH CUMULATIVE PERCENTAGE INCREASE OVER
THE FIVE YEAR PERIOD

	1966 Compensation	Cumulative Percentage Increase	1970 Compensation
Geographic			
West South Central	$ 8030	57	$12620
East South Central	9000	50	13500
West North Central	9900	43	14200
South Atlantic	10690	36	14570
Pacific	11850	35	16020
East North Central	11320	35	15310
Mid-Atlantic	12520	35	16940
Mountain	10500	32	13810
New England	14410	26	18210
Degree Levels			
Bachelor's	10570	36	14370
Limited Master's	11220	34	15000
Master's	11890	33	15970
Limited Doctor's	13000	33	17320
Doctor's	15410	30	20000
Enrollment Groups			
Largest	13790	38	19000
Smallest	8500	36	11580
Small	9960	35	11580

Table 18. *Continued*

Medium	11310	35	15260
Large	11850	34	15820

Denominational Groups (with at least 3 institutions reporting).

American Baptist			
Convention	9460	60	15110
Disciples of Christ	9500	52	14400
United Church of Christ	9750	51	14760
Seventh Day Adventist	6500	47	9540
Mennonite	7500	46	10920
United Presbyterian,			
U.S.A.	10530	41	14800
Church of the Brethren	8880	40	12430
Quaker	9940	37	13620
Southern Baptist	9000	36	12220
Lutheran Church in			
America	11270	35	15260
Methodist	10750	35	14510
Roman Catholic	11010	34	14710
Other	10490	32	13880
Presbyterian, U.S.	11300	31	14820
American Lutheran			
Church	11600	30	15080
Independent	13600	30	17700
Episcopal	14900	20	17960

Looking at professorial compensation by degree levels, the data indicate that the lower the degree, the higher the cumulative percentage increase in compensation. In dollar terms, however, the more complex the institution, the higher the compensation.

Even though compensation increased by a higher percentage in Bachelor's than in Doctor's institutions, because the dollar base was larger for more complex institutions, the dollar spread at the end of the period was greater among them than it had been at the beginning. The dollar difference between being a professor at a Bachelor's institution and a professor at a Doctor's institution was $4840 in 1966. In 1970, even though the cumulative percentage increase in compensation was 6 percent larger in the Bachelor's institution than in the Doctor's institution, the dollar difference had increased to $5630. That means an increase in the dollar gap of

$790 or 16 percent in just five years. With the exception of the gap between Bachelor's and Limited Master's institutions which remained virtually constant, the gap between each of the other groups widened by between $240 and $300.

The cumulative increase in the salary of professors by enrollment groups is similar in each group, ranging from 34 percent in the Large group to 38 percent in the Largest. In terms of dollars, however, the larger the institution—as grouped into the five enrollment groups—the higher the professor's compensation. In 1970 the average professor in the Smallest enrollment group received $11,580. His salary was exceeded 17 percent in the Small, 32 percent in the Medium, 37 percent in the Large, and 64 percent in the Largest. Indeed, the professor in the Largest enrollment group received 19 percent more at the start of the period in 1966 than his counterpart in the Smallest enrollment group did at the end of the period in 1970.

With the exception of Medium and Large, the dollar gap of compensation paid professors widened noticeably between enrollment groups over the five year period. It increased $480 between Smallest and Small, $390 between Small and Medium, $20 between Medium and Large, and $1240 between Large and Largest. The gap between compensation paid professors in the Smallest and that paid professors in the Largest increased from $5290 to $7420, or 40 percent.

The cumulative percentage increase of compensation for professors has been strikingly different from one denominational group to another. The increase has ranged from as low as 20 percent in institutions related to the Episcopal Church, to as high as 60 percent for American Baptist Convention schools. In dollar amounts, however, professors in Episcopalian-related institutions were still getting $2850 more at the end of the five-year period than professors in American Baptist-related institutions, but the gap had been cut in half (see Table 18).

Professors in Episcopalian-related institutions were more highly compensated than those in institutions related to any other denomination both in 1966 and still in 1970, despite the fact that the cumulative percentage increase in their compensation was the lowest of any denominational group. Professors in institutions related to the Seventh Day Adventist Church, despite the fact that the cumulative increase in their dollar compensation was the fourth highest of all the groups, were the most poorly compensated both at the start of the period and at the end. Indeed, because their very different cumulative increases proceed from such different bases, the dollar difference between professors in these two kinds of institutions is almost the same at the end of the period as at the beginning. But, instead of being paid nearly 2.3 times as much as his Seventh Day counterpart, the Episcopalian professor now receives only 1.88 times as much.

Compensation of the full professor rose a cumulative 35 percent over these years, from $11,280 to $15,200; the compensation of the associate professor rose 32 percent, from $9450 to $12,440; and that of the assistant professor rose 29 percent, from $8110 to $10,500. While the full professor received 39 percent more than the average assistant professor in 1966, his relatively faster increases rendered his 1970 compensation 45 percent greater than that received by the assistant professor. His compensation was 19 percent greater than the associate professor in 1966, but 22 percent greater by 1970.

One might have anticipated that assistant and associate professors should have gained on professors during these years. The supply of Ph.D.'s increased significantly but competition for them was keen and this was a period of large input at the lower ranks. If the natural market had been operating alone, the gap between the compensation of assistant professors, associate professors, and professors would have narrowed. The fact that it widened instead suggests that some other factor was at work. Perhaps it was the AAUP salary scales which emphasized compensation growth at the professorial level rather than at the lower ranks. Perhaps, too, as Kurt Hertzfeld notes (in private correspondence), the disappearance of the rank of instructor and the consequent downward pull on the compensation of the assistant professor was a contributing factor.

All of these percentage increases, however, are less than the total educational and general budget increases over the same period for which we have comparable data, and less than tuition and fee increases on a per student basis. Between 1968 and 1969, for example, the total educational and general budget increased 12.5

percent, instruction and departmental research increased 11.1 percent (9.7 percent on a per student basis), tuition income increased 10 percent on a per student basis, while compensation for professors increased only 7.6 percent.

In Doctor's institutions the dollar gap between assistant and associate professors widened by $600. The gap between associate professors and professors widened by $1440. Comparable figures for Largest institutions are $580 and $3190. Even in Small institutions, where the dollar amounts are smaller for all academic levels, the gap widened by $530 between assistant and associate professors, and by $750 between associate professors and professors.

Professors and associate professors cost an institution more than assistant professors and instructors. Presumably they are worth more. Full-time faculty members are also more costly than their equivalent in part time members who, in most cases, have some other major vocation which they complement with a little college teaching by moonlight. Again, presumably, full-time faculty contribute more to the total educational scene than their teaching equivalent in part-time persons. In a time of financial stringency, however, one might expect institutions to seek a mix of faculty that would emphasize the less costly members: lower ranks and part-time.

This is not what happened in private colleges and universities over the years covered by these data. As the institutions slid off the roof of surpluses and down the cellar door of deficits, the faculty distribution remained the same. These percentage distributions among upper and lower ranks and between full and part-time were set by a Mede or a Persian. They did not change. In 1966 assistant professors and instructors comprised 46 percent of the faculty in private institutions. In 1970 they still comprised 46 percent of the faculty. There was a very slight increase in full-time staff at the lecturer or teaching assistant level, apparently a result of employing as full-time staff a few who were formerly employed at that level on a part-time basis. Professors and associate professors wavered only two-tenths of 1 percent from their original 40 percent. Clearly, the faculty mix does not change easily. This has been the case, at least, as private colleges and universities passed through an expansionist era. As present faculty members age and few new young persons are added to the faculties, a shift toward the upper ranks seems likely. This will have a further unfavorable effect upon the financial status of private colleges and universities.

There were some changes evident in smaller groups of colleges. Among the small group of private colleges located in the Mountain region, for example, the percentage of their combined faculties made up of full and associate professors (full-time) increased 8.5 percentage points between 1966 and 1970. This was done by trimming the piece of pie formerly taken by assistant professors and instructors with a little sliver also taken off the "other" part-time teaching staff (a category which embraces lecturers and teaching assistants). In the East South Central region, by contrast, the opposite movement took place. The number of full-time assistant professors and instructors increased 9 percentage points, full-time professors and associate professors dropping 7.5 percentage points, with the remainder of the difference being taken at the expense of part-time people in various ranks. The next largest redistribution of faculty strength took place in the South Atlantic region where part-time persons lost 6.4 percentage points, largely to full-time professors (3.6 percentage points) and assistant professors and instructors (2.3 percentage points).

When institutional groupings were examined by enrollment levels, changes appeared in the percentages of part-time faculty and full-time assistant professors and instructors, but they were usually minor, commonly less than 2 percentage points. The largest change—a decrease in "other part-time faculty" of 4.5 percentage points—occurred in Medium institutions.

Institutional groupings by degree level also changed their distributions insignificantly among upper and lower ranks and between full- and part-time status. The largest percentage point change was a 3.1 increase in the percentage of assistant professors and instructors in Limited Master's institutions.

There was, in sum, very little change in the distribution of faculty by rank and by full- or part-time in any of the degree level groups of institutions. Individual institutions within a group can undergo significant changes, of course, but when these are offset by opposing changes in other individual institutions, the surface of the group is ruffled hardly at all.

Student-Faculty Ratio

One of the most important factors in the cost of instruction is the student-faculty ratio. To discover what these ratios were, the institutions in this study were asked what their ratios had been each year from 1966 through 1970. An examination of their responses seemed to indicate that their ratios were only reasonable approximations; they gave evidence of a "lingering" effect, as though a ratio was arrived at every two or three years and was considered valid until computed again. This method was too casual to provide data worthy of further analysis.

Therefore, we constructed our own student-faculty ratios using data from full-time/full-time equivalent students and full-time/full-time equivalent faculty. This gave a more consistent basis for comparisons among years. Because these data included two years of anticipated data, we could see what student-faculty ratios the colleges were, by implication, projecting.

The student-faculty ratio is a measure of productivity. Yet, to academic ears, the term "productivity" has such a coarse and dissonant sound that it is not merely unattractive but grating. Education is not like industry, which deals in output per unit of input. To call for measures of output, therefore, sounds as shrill in the halls of academe as would the use of a factory whistle to announce the end of each class period. What a man learns and, more importantly, what a man becomes, cannot, say academics, be very well measured in countable measures. Still less can these measures be arranged on an assembly line and accelerated.

Especially does this seem to be true with regard to the intimacy of contact between students and professors. Higher education, as William Baumol has pointed out, is a handicraft industry, a labor-intensive industry. What is new in democracy is old hat in higher education. The idealized student-faculty ratio popularized by James A. Garfield—"one man, one prof"—antedates one man, one vote by a good many years. Faculty members appear to believe—as though informed by instinct—that human learning proceeds best, perhaps only, if the contact between learner and learned is kept intimate. A student-faculty ratio that is small, therefore, is better than one that is large.

What, then, in view of the worsening condition of private higher education over the last several years, has been happening to the student-faculty ratio? It appears, in brief, to be going down; that is, the number of students taught per faculty member is declining. For the nation, the number of students per teacher was 12.6 in 1967. This declined to 11.7 by 1970, and projected data results in only a slight rise by 1972, to 11.9. The trend is the opposite of what one would expect to find in periods of financial stress, if student-faculty ratios were quickly responsive to financial need.

It is not altogether reasonable to argue that this ratio has been decreasing because institutions and their faculties have been proceeding in carefree disregard for their worsening financial condition. It is, in part, a consequence of a changing enrollment picture. Not only has the rate of enrollment increase declined to almost zero for all private institutions taken collectively, but the number enrolled has actually decreased in some institutions, while tenured faculty continue their employment. The ratio declined in part also because of a deliberate effort in some institutions to make the ratio more attractive to faculty as well as to students. The results of this effort were unfortunately beginning to be realized at the very time that enrollment increases began to fall off, thus accelerating the falling ratio and exacerbating the problem.

There is another reason for the declining ratio. The knowledge explosion put great pressure on institutions to expand their program offerings even if enrollment did not increase. Besides, convinced both that they would grow and that there was economy in growth, the institutions were caught anticipating an enrollment growth that could not be sustained. They were adding to the load in the basket at the very time the air began to go out of the balloon.

By regions in 1969–70, the highest student faculty ratio (14.8) appears in the West South Central region, the lowest (10.2) in the Mid-Atlantic region. In every region the ratio was a smaller figure than had obtained three years earlier and, in every instance but two, smaller than four years earlier. The average change for the regions over the three year period, 1966–67 to 1969–70, was a drop of approximately one full-time student in the student-faculty ratio. This amounts to a percentage change in the student faculty ratio of between 7 and 8 percent. A change of this magnitude, representing a decline in productivity, is reflected in the fiscal position of private colleges and universities. It is a measure of the underused instructional potential of these institutions.

Among denominational groups, the lowest student faculty ratio in 1969–70 was 9.8, set by institutions independent of church relationship and support. The highest ratio (18.5) was found in colleges related to the Quaker tradition. The ratios for all denominational groups are as in Table 19.

Table 19. STUDENT-FACULTY RATIOS: BY DENOMINATIONS: 1969–1970

Independent	9.8 to 1
Seventh Day Adventist	11.0
Roman Catholic	11.7
Episcopal	11.8
Disciples of Christ	13.2
Reformed Church in America	13.7
Methodist	14.0
Mennonite	14.0
Church of the Brethren	14.1
United Church of Christ	14.4
Lutheran Church in America	14.6
United Presbyterian, U.S.A.	14.8
American Baptist Convention	15.1
Southern Baptist	15.3
American Lutheran Church	15.3
Presbyterian, U.S.	16.0
Other	16.0
Church of the Nazarene	17.0
Church of Christ	17.9
Quaker	18.5

Student-faculty ratios also differ at various enrollment levels. There appears to be, moreover, a relationship between the fiscal fortunes of the enrollment groups and their student-faculty ratios. Both the Smallest and the Largest institutions have a low student-faculty ratio (probably for very different reasons) and both have the most severe financial problems. Their ratios are, respectively,

9.3 and 9.4. The group of institutions relatively more stable financially, the Large institutions, has the highest ratio of 14.5, followed by 13.6 for Medium institutions, and 12.4 for Small institutions. All enrollment groups hoped to increase that ratio in the next couple of years. All, that is, except the Largest. The institutions in that group expected no change.

The highest ratio when the institutions are grouped by degree levels is found among the Limited Master's institutions. Their ratio is 14.7. Second highest at 13.9 is the group of Bachelor's institutions. This group is followed by Master's institutions (13.4), Limited Doctor's (10.1), and Doctor's (7.7). Thus, with the exception of institutions that include a very few masters degree programs in their offerings, the higher the degree level and the more complex the institution, the lower the student-faculty ratio. Limited Master's institutions have nearly twice as many students per faculty member as Doctors institutions.

It may be useful to add that the group of Limited Master's institutions does not correspond to any enrollment group. It draws less than 20 percent of its membership from the enrollment group (Large) with the highest student-faculty ratio, and less than half from the enrollment group (Medium) with the second highest. Both of those enrollment groups have a lower ratio than the Limited Master's group. Some factor other than size is operating in this degree level group.

Efforts to relate student-faculty ratios directly to deficit and surplus levels of operation are not fully satisfactory. We arranged institutions in order from greatest degree of deficit as a percentage of current fund budget to least degree of deficit; and from least degree of surplus to greatest degree of surplus; and we divided both deficit and surplus groups into quartiles. We discovered within each quartile a wide range of student faculty ratios. It is quite possible for two institutions with the same student faculty ratio to find themselves at opposite ends of the deficit to surplus spectrum. In order to prevent a few very large institutions from washing out distinctions among institutions, each institution was assigned an equal weight. The ratios within each surplus and deficit quartile were averaged and Figure 5 was produced.

The group of institutions in the quartile of greatest degree

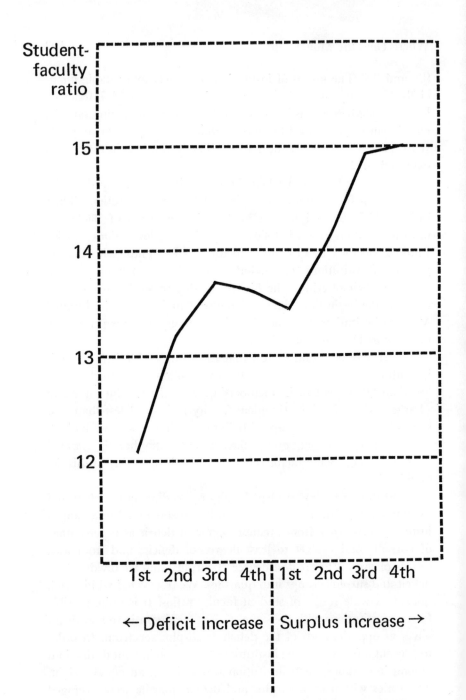

FIGURE 5. Student-faculty ratios and deficit/surplus budget institutions, 1969–70.

of deficit has a student faculty ratio of 12.1. The group of institutions in the quartile of greatest degree of surplus has a student faculty ratio of 15.0. Without demonstrating which came first, the deficit/surplus or the student faculty ratio, the line does suggest some correlation between the two.

Another analysis can be made within each enrollment group. The student-faculty ratio difference between surplus and deficit institutions becomes especially noticeable in groups with the largest sized institutions. While Largest institutions running surpluses had a ratio of 16.9, those running deficits had a ratio of only 13.3. In the Large group the surplus institutions averaged 16.7 while the deficit institutions averaged 15.2. Among smaller groups the difference between surplus and deficit institutions was marginal.

Student faculty ratios by size of budget, deserve a concluding comment. If, again, the size of the budget grouping is judged by its own weighting, we may average the ratios of the institutions within each budget range to discover an average ratio. Visually this would present a peak student faculty ratio of 15.1 for the group of institutions in the six to eight million dollar budget range, with a slope on either side of this peak; whether moving toward a higher or a lower budget range, one moves to a lower student faculty ratio. It declines to 12.2 for institutions with a budget above fifteen million, and falls all the way to 9.7 for institutions with a budget under one million dollars.

Expenditures per Student

This is a good point at which to discuss costs, or expenditures, per student and to see if some comparisons can be made among institutions by size. It is frequently alleged that small institutions are in severe difficulty because they are uneconomical: the overall cost per student is greater in small institutions than large institutions. A period of financial stress uncovers this basic weakness in the economic stamina of small colleges which a less arduous time might conceal. Since they are too costly to be self-supporting, runs the argument, and too fiscally inefficient to deserve outside support, an economy minded age cannot afford them. It is better that they pass from the scene, with nostalgia perhaps, but pass nevertheless.

The financial and enrollment data gathered in this study do not substantiate the bald assertion that small colleges are inherently uneconomical, or that large institutions are economical.

We examined expenditure data for each of the five enrollment groups both on a full-time equivalent student basis and on a student head count basis, employing only institutions able to supply complete expenditure and enrollment data for 1968 and 1969. Under the expense heading Instruction and Departmental Research (faculty salaries, largely), in terms of full-time equivalent enrollment, the data for both years shows that Small institutions (between 501–1000) average the lowest expenditure per student of any enrollment group. An institution enrolling less than one thousand students is, in virtually everyone's lexicon, a small college. Large institutions (between 2001–4000), however, have the next lowest. In 1968, third place was a toss-up between Smallest institutions (500 students or less) and Medium institutions (1001–2000). In 1969, however, third place clearly went to the Medium group. Fifth place is held by the group of Largest institutions. The picture is slightly different in terms of total head count enrollment. The contest for lowest expenditure per student is between Small institutions and Large institutions with the former winning in 1968, the latter in 1969. Third place is securely held both years by the Smallest institutions. Fourth place goes to Medium institutions and last place goes to the Largest institutions.

That this order is not simply the result of the student-faculty ratio may be seen in Table 20. The one group significantly out of place is the Small group. It has a student-faculty ratio smaller than

Table 20.   STUDENT-FACULTY RATIOS AND COST PER STUDENT: BY ENROLLMENT SIZE: 1968 AND 1969

Student-faculty ratio		Instructional expenditure per student	
(Full-time equivalency)			
Smallest	9.3	Small	$ 878
Largest	9.4	Large	$ 917
Small	12.4	Medium	$ 953
Medium	13.6	Smallest	$ 972
Large	14.5	Largest	$1333

the Medium and Large groups but the lowest expenditure per student for instruction.

These rankings based on instruction and departmental research expenditures do not change if we arbitrarily assign all graduate students a weight of two in partial acknowledgement that additional expense is involved in graduate education. Nor do they change if students are treated on a full-time equivalent basis. On a head count basis, the chief difference is that Largest institutions average an expenditure per student that moves them into fourth place in 1968 and third place in 1969. First place goes to the Large group, second place to the Small group, fourth place to the Medium group, and slipping from third place to fifth in one year's time, the Smallest group.

The range on a full-time equivalent basis for instruction and departmental research in 1968 is from $801 per student in Small institutions to $1235 at Largest institutions. On a head count basis the range is from $751 to $967 in the same two groups of institutions.

When graduate students get a weight of two, the range in 1968 is from $797 to $1012 per student in the same two groups on a full-time equivalent student basis. On a head count basis the range is from $714 for the Large group, to $790 for the Medium group. These data are set forth in Table 21.

The other principal expenditure category in the educational and general account is General Administration (student services, staff benefits, general institutional expenses), and with these figures, it appears that larger institutions have an advantage over the smaller. Again, however, it is not the very largest which have the lowest average expenditure per student (on a full-time equivalent basis) but the Large group. The Largest group has the second lowest by this reckoning, and the lowest on a head count basis or when graduate students are given a weight of two. Third is the Medium group. The Small group is fourth, and the Smallest group is fifth. There appear to be certain basic expenses involved in the administration of an institution of higher learning which, in a small institution, are reflected in a higher expenditure per student than at a larger institution. The Smallest group indicates the severity of this trend: the spread between the other four groups in 1969 on a full-

Table 21. COMPARISON OF INSTRUCTION AND DEPARTMENTAL RESEARCH EXPENDITURES PER STUDENT: BY ENROLLMENT GROUPS: 1968 AND 1969

	Smallest	Small	Medium	Large	Largest
1968, Full-Time-Equivalent Basis	$877	$801	$876	$857	$1234
1969, Full-Time-Equivalent Basis	972	878	953	917	1333
Change	+95	+77	+77	+60	+99
1968, Head-Count Basis	$782	$751	$816	$756	$ 967
1969, Head-Count Basis	874	827	889	808	1055
Change	+92	+45	+73	+52	+88
Each Graduate Student Valued at Twice Each Undergraduate:					
1968, Full-Time-Equivalent Basis	$869	$797	$860	$824	$1012
1969, Full-Time-Equivalent Basis	962	873	935	877	1093
Change	+93	+76	+75	+53	+81
1968, Head-Count Basis	$772	$744	$790	$714	$ 781
1969, Head-Count Basis	863	818	860	760	850
Change	+91	+74	+70	+46	+69

Table 22. COMPARISON OF GENERAL ADMINISTRATION EXPENDITURES PER STUDENT:
BY ENROLLMENT GROUPS: 1968 AND 1969

	Smallest	Small	Medium	Large	Largest
1968, Full-Time-Equivalent Basis	$608	$516	$514	$452	$467
1969, Full-Time-Equivalent Basis	715	593	575	511	527
Change	+107	+77	+61	+59	+60
1968, Head-Count Basis	$543	$484	$479	$399	$366
1969, Head-Count Basis	644	559	537	450	417
Change	+101	+75	+58	+51	+51
Each Graduate Student Valued at Twice Each Undergraduate:					
1968, Full-Time-Equivalent Basis	$603	$513	$505	$435	$383
1969, Full-Time-Equivalent Basis	708	590	564	489	432
Change	+105	+77	+59	+54	+49
1968, Head-Count Basis	$536	$479	$464	$377	$295
1969, Head-Count Basis	635	553	519	423	336
Change	+99	+74	+55	+46	+41

time equivalent student basis is $82, but the jump from the Small-est group to the Small group is $122. These figures are set forth in Table 22. Note, in examining this table that the increase in adminis-trative cost from 1968 to 1969 is inversely related to size.

The Educational and General account (see Table 23) is the basic educational account of the college. It includes both Instruction and Departmental Research expenditures and General Administra-tion costs. For all private institutions the former is about 50 percent of the Educational and General budget; the latter about 25 percent. That leaves another 25 percent, which includes such items as the running of the library, operating and maintaining physical plant, and various other relatively small expenditures common to most institutions of higher learning. (Educational and General also in-cludes sponsored research and medical center expenditures if any. To facilitate cost comparisons on a per student basis, these two items have been eliminated from the analyses that follow. Hospitals and medical schools are not typical of all of private higher educa-tion, and sponsored research is both atypical and generates off-set-ting sources of income which, for the years covered by the study, actually exceeded expenditures.)

Because Small institutions (in second place) do almost as well as Large institutions (in first place)—followed by Medium, Largest, and Smallest—for this remaining 25 percent of Educa-tional and General expenditures, they came out in 1968 (on a full-time-equivalent student basis) with the lowest average cost per student for all Educational and General expenditures. Large institu-tions had the second lowest. In 1969 (and also, on a head-count basis, 1968) the positions were reversed. In third place in both years and whether reckoned on a full-time or a head-count basis was the Medium group. In fourth place—on a full-time-equivalent student basis—the Smallest group, and in fifth place, the Largest group. On a head-count basis these last two groups reversed positions.

When graduate students are given the weight of two, the position of the groups remains about the same on a full-time-equivalent student basis. On a head-count basis, however, doubling the large numbers of part-time graduate students dramatically shuffles the order. On a head-count basis in 1969, the larger the enrollment size, the lower the average expenditure per student.

Table 23. COMPARISONS OF EDUCATIONAL AND GENERAL (LESS SPONSORED RESEARCH AND MEDICAL CENTER) EXPENDITURES PER STUDENT BY ENROLLMENT GROUPS: 1968 AND 1969

	Smallest	Small	Medium	Large	Largest
1968, Full-Time-Equivalent Basis	$1999	$1736	$1829	$1755	$2234
1969, Full-Time-Equivalent Basis	2254	1936	1996	1894	2451
Change	+255	+200	+167	+139	+217
1968, Head-Count Basis	$1783	$1627	$1704	$1549	$1750
1969, Head-Count Basis	2028	1824	1863	1670	1939
Change	+245	+197	+159	+121	+189
Each Graduate Student Valued at Twice Each Undergraduate:					
1968, Full-Time-Equivalent Basis	$1981	$1726	$1796	$1687	$1831
1969, Full-Time-Equivalent Basis	2232	1925	1959	1812	2011
Change	+62	+199	+163	+125	+180
1968, Head-Count Basis	$1760	$1610	$1650	$1463	$1413
1969, Head-Count Basis	2002	1803	1803	1569	1564
Change	+242	+193	+153	+106	+151

These analyses do not look deeply into the complexity of determining cost per student by type of program and by level of student. Sophisticated projects elsewhere will now develop formulae for these analyses. This problem might be approached by assigning graduate students a weight greater than that of undergraduates, which we have done. It should be noted, however, that any weight is more or less arbitrary, and the weight should ordinarily be higher for doctoral degree students than for those seeking the masters degree. Since our enrollment groups do not distinguish between enrollments for master's, doctor's, and professional degrees, we assigned all graduate students a weight double that of undergraduates. Assigning graduate students a weight of two is probably adequate for comparing master's degree education with undergraduate education, but inadequate for comparing many doctoral programs with baccalaureate education. It must be added, too, that the word *small* is very elastic and can be stretched to suit the user's own lexicon. It may be that some consider small even an institution of 8500—the approximate average size in 1968 of the institutions in our largest enrollment group.

Finally, questions of quality of education, of comparability of education, of services rendered, are not examined—let alone answered—by these data. No attempt has been made in these analyses to evaluate the type of program being offered or the extent to which it is enriched. Small colleges that show themselves economical in these analyses are not apt to be offering a wide range of educational opportunities. The very narrowness of their offerings, in fact, makes their competition with larger institutions difficult. It is legitimate to note, however, that not all students may want or need available the variety of educational offerings available at large institutions. Considering the programs they offer, in conjunction with differences in consumer tastes, we cannot conclude that small colleges are inherently uneconomical. For the enrollment ranges used here and for the expenditure items examined, it simply cannot be said baldly that "the trouble with the small college is that it is uneconomical." One group of small colleges appears to be relatively economical; another considerably less so. A lot depends upon what you mean by small, what you mean by economical, and how you define quality in an educational program. It is well to keep in mind, further, that tastes vary and that consumer satisfaction can more nearly be maximized if different groups are able to approximate closely the particular type of education they desire.

Physical Plant Expenditures

The operation and maintenance of the physical plant constitutes a major burden in the operation of an institution of higher learning. Students, their professors, and the equipment they use— a plant item itself—all require adequate facilities. This one item accounts for twelve cents out of every educational and general dollar spent by private colleges and universities (ranging from a low of 10.3 for institutions in the Pacific region to a high of 12.9 in the New England region). In terms of size, as we have noted, the smaller the institution, the larger the percentage of its educational and general budget it must devote to this purpose. Smallest institutions devote 16 percent of their budget to this purpose, while Largest institutions devote only 11.3 percent (minus sponsored research and medical center) of theirs. The complexity of the institution, however, appears to have little effect on the percentage spent on the physical plant: Bachelor's institutions spend 12.7 percent, Doctor's institutions spend 11.4 percent.

The flow of decreasing percentages for operation and maintenance of physical plant as the size of the institutions increases is not, of course, mirrored in the total dollar amounts expended. The average Smallest institution spent $114,000 on this category of expenses in 1969; the average Largest institution spent $1,864,000. The flow is reversed on a per student basis also. The Largest group, although it spent least as a percentage of its budget, spent the second largest amount per student. Per student, Smallest spent $307, Small spent $226, Medium spent $226, Large spent $213, and Largest spent $268.

The operation and maintenance of physical plant takes such a large chunk out of the educational and general budget in part because colleges and universities have a very substantial investment in plant and equipment. The average book value of the physical plant of a private college or university is over fifteen million dollars, or eleven and a half billion dollars for all private accredited four-year colleges and universities. That represents a lot of bricks and mortar. It is, moreover, just the book value figure; this is the amount of money actually invested in the plant, original cost plus money spent on additions or changes. The value if measured in market or in replacement terms would be very much larger. Book value, however, has the convenience of being the most commonly kept figure and hence one we could be sure of obtaining from almost every institution.

The smaller the institution, the lower the value of the physical plant (Table 24). On a per student basis, however, as judged by the median institution, the smaller the institution, the higher the value of the plant. The same phenomenon is not at work when institutions are examined by degree levels. Doctors institutions have the largest median value per student as well as the largest average dollar value per institution.

Table 24. VALUE OF PHYSICAL PLANT: AVERAGE BOOK VALUE
AND PER STUDENT VALUE: 1969

	Average Institution (in millions)	Per Student (full-time equivalent)
Enrollment Groups		
Smallest	$ 3.5	$9,230
Small	6.7	8,350
Medium	10.8	7,660
Large	17.9	6,960
Largest	57.8	5,590
Degree Levels		
Bachelor's	$ 8.0	$7,800
Limited Master's	12.2	7,470
Master's	14.7	6,680
Limited Doctor's	32.4	7,430
Doctor's	74.7	10,820

Among other things, these figures seem to make two obvious points. One is that, as residential colleges have typically been conceived, a certain basic investment in plant is required. As an institution grows larger it does not have to replicate each segment of that plant for each additional student. One football field will do as well for a large student body as for a small one. It does need to be ten yards longer for each 100 students. The other is that plant costs per student are higher among doctoral granting universities than at less complex institutions even though universities are also typically larger than less complex institutions. Costs are higher because graduate instruction requires more space and more expensive equipment and also, perhaps, because many private universities have physical properties that are among the most elegant in the nation. There are private universities that have a per student book value of physical plant as high as $38,000. However, there is also a private college with a per student book value of less than $1,000.

Geography—provided enough institutions are represented in each region—tends to smooth out sharp differences. The per student plant values of the median institutions in regions in the East, however, are higher than elsewhere in the country. New England, Mid-Atlantic, East North Central and South Atlantic regions are in the eight-thousand dollar range. The Pacific and West North Central regions are in the seven-thousand dollar range, while the West South Central, East South Central, and Mountain regions are in the six-thousand dollar range.

Denominational groups have substantially different plant book values on a per student reckoning. Episcopalians, at $18,450, are in a class by themselves. Southern Presbyterians (Presbyterian Church, U.S.) at $10,080 per student have second billing, followed by those independent of church relationship with $9090. Next comes Roman Catholic colleges at $8210. Arranged in descending order, the median book values of the physical plants of denominational groups on a full-time-equivalent basis are as follows:

Episcopal	$18,450
Presbyterian, U.S.	10,080
Independent	9,090
Roman Catholic	8,210
American Baptist Convention	8,030
Lutheran Church in America	7,720
United Presbyterian, U.S.A.	7,530
Methodist	7,480
Reformed Church in America	6,980
Southern Baptist	6,880

American Lutheran Church	6,810
United Church of Christ	6,620
Disciples of Christ	6,340
Seventh Day Adventist	6,080
Other	6,070
Church of Christ	5,840
Mennonite	5,680
Church of the Nazarene	5,340
Quaker	5,060

Indebtedness on Physical Plant

A substantial amount of the plant is new and unpaid for. This speaks well in terms of its present utility and condition but not in terms of debt service payments. Private colleges and universities are in debt for over a quarter (26 percent) of the book value of their physical plants. In dollars this amounts to over three billion dollars of indebtedness on the physical plant, an average of four million dollars per institution. Over half (51 percent) of this indebtedness is to the federal government. Slightly under one-eighth (12 percent) is to themselves: institutions have borrowed from their own endowment and current funds. Over a quarter (26 percent) of their indebtedness on physical plant is to private sources of funding, 10 percent to state government, and a minuscule fraction (0.1 percent) to local government.

How one interprets these figures will depend in part on how one views the economic future of these debtors and the degrees of beneficence with which one believes their creditors will act in the event of a declining or failing return on their investment.

Two of the more interesting creditors are the federal government and the institution itself. Relatively few institutions have actually defaulted on federal loans, but several have been forced to ask for some concession, a moratorium on the payment of principal, for example; and some of those in actual default have not recovered their ability to resume debt service payments. The federal government has only difficult choices in these instances.

I have heard of the president of a small private college whose building program in recent years has placed the institution in debt on its physical plant for two-thirds of its value (nearly $8,000 per student) who believes that one day the federal government will forgive all of these outstanding loans. He has since retired and the institution recently hired another president, one committed to the repayment of these loans.

The indebtedness to other institutional funds is also interesting. The institution borrows from itself for the same reasons you and I may pay cash for a purchase rather than buy it on time: we find that we can lend ourselves the money at a cheaper rate than we can borrow it elsewhere. While an institution that uses money it could otherwise invest at, say, 5 percent to save borrowing at 8 percent nets a clear gain in the transaction, it has engaged in some incestuous financing that could have very serious implications in the event of further curtailment of income. Being a bad debtor to oneself means that one has already drawn on reserves to which one might turn in a reversal and has no one to sue for recovery. Moreover, the borrowed funds, on which interest is seldom paid, are sterilized as an investment. This sterilization is important in computing the strength of the institution's endowment. One might assume a growth rate and income-earning rate that would improve the endowment and its ability to be used for program functions, but not if it is committed to a noninterest or niggardly-interest loan. The old saw about the man who serves as his own legal advisor having a fool for a client and a dunce for a lawyer may apply with milder force to the institution that borrows from itself too heavily.

The picture of relative indebtedness is not the same for all institutions and for all parts of the country. The degree of indebtedness on physical plant (book value) changes in different regions from 19 percent in New England to 33 percent in the western Mountain region. It ranges from a low of about 20 percent for Doctor's universities to approximately 30 percent for Bachelor's and Limited Master's institutions. In general, the higher the level of degree offering, the lower the degree of indebtedness on the book value of physical plant.

Among denominational groups plant indebtedness varies from 21 percent to 45 percent. Independent (non-church-related) institutions at 25 percent have a low degree of indebtedness on physical plant and the largest denominational group of church-related institutions, Roman Catholic, have a lower ratio still, 24 percent.

The extent to which denominational groups have turned to the federal government for loans on their physical plant is especially interesting. The breadth of that range is most tellingly illustrated by the data on three denominations: the Seventh Day Adventist, the Mennonite, and the United Church of Christ. These three have in common the fact that the degree of indebtedness on their physical plants is, for each of them, 37 and a fraction percent. The percentage of that indebtedness that is owed to the federal government is, however, quite different. For Seventh Day Adventists it is zero percent; for the Mennonites it is 28 percent; and for the United Church of Christ it is 74 percent.

The denominationally related group of colleges with the highest indebtedness is the Nazarene Church group with 45 percent. The denominational group with the lowest plant indebtedness is the Southern Baptist Church colleges group at 21 percent. The percentage of that indebtedness owed to the federal government, however, is 69 percent for both the Nazarene and Southern Baptist colleges.

Indebtedness on the physical plant on a per student basis ranges all the way from one college carrying ten dollars of debt for each full-time equivalent student to one carrying a staggering $14,285 for each student. With such a vast range, the median figures used are much like the fulcrum of a long and unwieldy teeter-totter. By indicating the point at which the balance is struck, however, they are useful for establishing comparisons among groups.

By enrollment levels, the smaller the institution, the larger the median figure of indebtedness per full-time equivalent student. As the following figures indicate, smaller schools simply have fewer backs upon which to distribute the load. Median indebtedness per student for the enrollment groups are:

Smallest	$3320
Small	2560
Medium	2330
Large	2130
Largest	1670

By degree levels, Bachelor's institutions have the highest median plant debt figure of any group, followed by the Limited Doctor's group. The largest amount of debt per student for any institution in the Limited Doctor's group ($4270), however, is exceeded by 42 colleges in the Bachelor's group. The median debt figures per student for each degree level group are:

Bachelor's	$2580
Limited Master's	2280
Master's	1710
Limited Doctor's	2300
Doctor's	1920

Indebtedness, judged on a median per student basis, is not evenly distributed across the country. There is, moreover, a rough correlation between plant value and plant indebtedness. The New England region which has the highest median plant value also carries the highest median indebtedness per student ($2790), and the Mid-Atlantic region is in second place in both categories. Individual institutions, however, may veer wildly from the course. Thus, one institution with a plant value of nearly $39,000 per student carries a plant indebtedness of slightly over $1800 per student. Institutions in the three Southern regions have the lowest median plant indebtedness, from $1560 to $1840 per student.

While there are some instances of marked correlation among denominational groups between median per student plant value and median per student plant indebtedness (the Episcopal and Presbyterian, U.S. churches lead both lists; the Quakers are at the bottom of both) there are also some notable exceptions. Mennonites, for example, have a relatively low median plant value and a relatively high indebtedness figure. Roman Catholic and Southern Baptist colleges, on the other hand, have relatively higher plant value figures compared with their standing in a scale of per student plant indebtedness.

The indebtedness on new plant, both academic facilities and auxiliary enterprises, has two cost implications. The one is present, the other future. The present one is the load on the current fund operation to retire the debt on these buildings. The future one is

the apparition of the next financial crisis: the renovation and replacement of these buildings.

While, in accordance with recommended accounting practice in effect at that time, the educational and general account
should not normally have included debt service payments, we asked
that it be included in this accounting. This should, of course, be
debt service on academic facilities only; debt service on auxiliary
enterprises should be subsumed under that account. Since the bulk
(approximately 86 percent) of the physical plant indebtedness (to
the federal government, at least) is for housing, the bulk of the
debt service on this indebtedness would therefore be found in the
Auxiliary Enterprises account. (This percentage may be changing.
A study of colleges in the state of Pennsylvania found that about
half of recent plant indebtedness was for educational facilities.)

We did not, however, ask that debt service (repayment of
principal and interest) on educational facilities be isolated as a
discrete item. It may, therefore, be entered either under operation
and maintenance of physical plant or under general administration,
or it may not have been entered at all. It is therefore unfortunate
but likely that the effect of debt service on current operations is
understated in these reckonings.

An average debt service percentage is not easily uncovered.
A study prepared for North Carolina institutions found a range
from 1.6 to 9.5, with the average at 4.0 percent. A carefully
weighted formula combining Office of Education and Housing
and Urban Development data works out, ultimately, to a 5.6 percent average on federal bonds for academic facilities and auxiliary
enterprises. At that rate, the average private institution with an
indebtedness on plant of $4,031,000 would have an average annual
debt service payment of $225,736. That would have meant, in
1969, an average of nearly $130 per full-time-equivalent student.

Since slightly better than half the total indebtedness on
physical plant is to the federal government, the debt service payment on federal loans would have been about $114,000, which is
almost within reach of the deficit ($131,000) incurred by this same
average institution in 1970. It has, therefore, occurred to some
institutions running deficits—including those 85 institutions that by

the end of calendar year 1972 were in some degree of difficulty on payments for college housing—to suggest that a moratorium on debt service payments to the federal government might be an expeditious form of direct federal aid. An institution already granted a favorable loan would be granted another favor.

There is precedent for the action, one of the most recent instances being the legislation passed in 1970 which went beyond a mere moratorium and eliminated interest charges altogether on the St. Lawrence Seaway bonded debts as a "practical, expedient method of dealing with a problem of considerable proportion." This action relieved the pressure for higher tolls, a tariff analogous to tuition in a private college.

We wondered, therefore, how a moratorium would affect institutions running deficits. We calculated the debt service payment to the federal government for each institution actually running a deficit and then calculated what percentage of the deficit would be met by a federal debt service moratorium. After one subtracts the forty-nine institutions that ran a deficit in 1969 but that recorded no indebtedness to the federal government, two-thirds of the remaining 188 had a debt service payment that was 50 percent or more of the deficit incurred by the institution that year. Most of these (76) were Bachelor's institutions, which is about a quarter of all the Bachelor's institutions in this study. Other degree and enrollment level groups were similarly represented, varying from a high of 29 percent of the Large group to 20 percent of the Largest group. For the Smallest group, however, only 9 percent were in this category. A moratorium on federal debt service, in other words, would be of less benefit to that group than to others.

A moratorium would create several problems. If it was general it would benefit the needy and not-so-needy alike and it would miss some needy ones. If it was not general it would require a sophisticated analysis of need in each individual case. It would also weaken what has been a strong argument for higher education in its search for federal support. One of higher education's proudest claims when it requested passage of the Academic Facilities Act in 1962–63 was that in not one case had the colleges defaulted on their dormitory obligations. This can no longer be said. However, it is still important to institutions wanting to borrow more money to be able to demonstrate the security in loans granted to institutions of higher learning.

The new plant has implications for the future as well as for the present. This plant will have to be renovated and, ultimately, replaced. Yet, beyond Hans Jenny[1] and a few others, no one seems to be doing much worrying about the fiscal implications of this future problem. The answer to this problem in the business world is depreciation. A charge is levied against the business income sufficient to provide the funds necessary for renovation and replacement of plant and equipment. This has not been common practice in higher education. Institutions of higher learning have acted as though there were something immoral about asking the present generation of students to pay a charge for buildings to be used by a future generation. Besides, capital gifts have been among the easiest funds to raise. (Renovation funds are another story. The donor does not get the same measure of satisfaction from a renovated facility as he does from a new one, complete with identifying plaque.)

There is another reason why depreciation has been more appropriate for business and industry than for higher education: taxation. Tax laws permit commercial enterprises to make a deduction for depreciation. Institutions of higher learning, which have not been subject to taxation, have not felt the same need. To raise the spectre of local taxation in order to ask what some of its implications might be and to make intelligent preparation against the possibility is like raising the subject of death at a dinner party. It is at least in bad taste and, to the superstitious, probably worse.

But what if colleges and universities were no longer unlike business in this respect? What if they were taxed? Then the practice of assigning depreciation allowance to plant and equipment would not only be prudent but necessary.

There are additional reasons why this practice may make increasing sense in the future. One is that private colleges and universities need to place emphasis in their development programs on raising money for current operations. This emphasis ought not be weakened by the present eagerness of donor and college president

---

[1] Hans H. Jenny and G. Richard Wynn, *The Turning Point* (Wooster, Ohio, 1972), pp. 52–54.

alike to yield to the temptation to leave concrete memorials to themselves. As long as there are regular building campaigns, the average donor and the average president will prefer to put money and effort into these than into campaigns for funds for operating expenses.

There is also this to consider: many private colleges do not need more new buildings, certainly not as many as they needed—or thought that they needed—in the decade of the sixties. Unless wise state legislators make it financially equitable for private colleges to expand, their enrollment bubble has burst. They do not, as a group, need more space. Edifice is no longer king.

Individual colleges, especially those that are late in developing their campuses, still need a building or two. One problem with academic space is that it is seldom interchangeable. It must be appropriate space, not mere space. An empty classroom simply will not pinch hit for a science laboratory, nor a seminar room for an auditorium. The fact that students are occupying the president's office does not necessarily mean that spaces in the library have opened as a result. And all colleges will need better space and, especially, ever more sophisticated equipment. But the emphasis in buildings should be on repair, renovation, rebuilding, and replacement, not on additions. Renovation and replacement are part of the cost of doing business. It will be prudent to have this cost reflected in the accounting structure through the assignment of depreciation allowances.

At present, however, the practice of setting aside depreciation allowance is not widespread and sometimes is not very realistic where it is practiced. Among our respondents it has been more widely practiced with regard to auxiliary enterprises—in large measure because some loan programs have required it—than with regard to academic facilities. Even here, however, only 17 percent of the responding private colleges and universities report that it has been their practice to set aside depreciation reserves on auxiliary enterprises, and only 14 percent indicate that they are presently setting aside these reserves. Only 9 percent have established the practice of setting aside depreciation reserves on educational and general plant; only 7 percent are presently doing so.

What if the renovation, renewal, and replacement dollar is

not forthcoming and institutions must turn to current operations to supply those funds? Could any institution of higher learning show a surplus if it had to start setting aside depreciation reserves to accomplish these tasks? The replacement cost of a bulding, according to a common formula, is figured at a rate of increase *over* original cost of 8 percent *per year*. If the book value of our average institution (fifteen million dollars) represented current value—which it does not, not by several million dollars—its replacement cost would increase by $1,200,000 during this year alone. No private institution is thinking in terms of sums of this magnitude.

General Administration Expenditures

The money also goes for such items as general administration: administrative expenses for the institution as a whole in contrast to smaller organizational units; student services: a large bag of unwieldy growing expenses including counseling, placement, health care; staff benefits: compensation other than salary which faculty members and others receive; and general institutional expenses: expenses on activities and offices serving the institution as a whole and not covered elsewhere in this accounting, including interest payments on current funds. Collectively these comprise an expenditure category of large dimensions.

For all private institutions taken together, they account for a quarter of the educational and general budget, exclusive of sponsored research and medical center expenses. By enrollment groups, the smaller the institution, the higher the percentage spent on this set of expenditure items. Similarly, the less complex the institution, the higher the percentage.

On a per student basis, then, the cost of these activities is lowest in the Large group. The order proceeds to the Largest group as next lowest, then the Medium group, followed closely by the Small group, and, bringing up the rear, the Smallest group.

By degree levels, the lowest cost per full-time equivalent student is the Limited Doctor's group; the highest is in the Doctor's group. There is a very close approximation between the dollar figure which is the average for the group as a whole and the dollar figure for the median institution in the group, as Table 25 indicates.

Table 25. GENERAL ADMINISTRATIVE, STUDENT SERVICES, STAFF BENEFITS, AND GENERAL INSTITUTIONAL EXPENSES: 1969

	Average Expenditure per Student for the Group	Average Expenditure per Student, Median Institution	Percentage of Educational and General Budget, (Exclusive of Sponsored Research and Medical Center)
Enrollment Groups			*percent*
Smallest	$715	$655	30.6
Small	593	541	30.5
Medium	575	540	28.3
Large	511	438	27.0
Largest	527	462	21.3
Degree Levels			
Bachelor's	$544	$531	30.1
Limited Master's	497	502	27.1
Master's	494	516	26.1
Limited Doctor's	484	486	22.9
Doctor's	638	630	21.0

By geographic analysis, five regions have an expenditure per student for this set of items in the $500 range. The New England and Mountain regions are relatively high in the $660's; while East South Central at $490 and West South Central just under $400 are relatively low. Among denominational groups, those related to the Episcopalian Church are high at $845; those related to the Nazarene's are low at $390. The Southern Baptist, Quaker, Other, Seventh Day Adventist, and Roman Catholic-related colleges are all less than $450 per student on this item. Besides the colleges related to the Episcopalian Church, only the United Church of Christ at $580 and those independent of church relationship at $645 are higher than $550.

Included within this set of expenditure items under general institutional expenses would be interest paid on current fund indebtedness. We looked a little more closely at this item to discover the sources to which these institutions are indebted. The total current fund indebtedness for all private institutions in 1969 was nearly half a billion dollars. The bulk (42.7 percent) was owed to current account payable and accrued taxes. Insignificant amounts were owed to local and state governments, but 5.1 percent was listed as owed to the federal government for "other than accrued payroll and other taxes." The remaining half was split nearly equally between private sources outside the institution, notes payable other than current accounts payable (27.6 percent) and other funds of the institution (24.1 percent).

These percentages are quite different from one enrollment group to another. Smaller institutions tend to have more of their current fund indebtedness committed to private sources (other than current accounts payable) than larger institutions. The bulk of the current fund indebtedness of larger institutions tends to be to current accounts payable and accrued taxes. See Table 26.

Table 26. CURRENT FUND INDEBTEDNESS: 1969

	Average Current Fund Indebtedness	Percentage Owed Other Funds of the Institution	Percentage Owed Private Sources
Smallest	$ 233,000	39	38
Small	248,000	29	41
Medium	397,000	15	39
Large	617,000	23	26
Largest	3,160,000	26	20

Examined by degree levels the data indicate that approximately one-third of the current fund indebtedness at baccalaureate and Master's degree institutions is to private sources, notes payable, while in universities granting the doctorate it is one-fifth. One-quarter of the indebtedness in Bachelor's institutions and in Doctor's institutions is to other funds of the institution.

In determining the significance of current fund indebtedness for the financial health of the institution, the amount of that indebtedness relative to the strength of the institution and the terms under which loans are obtained are among the more critical factors. The distribution of that indebtedness is an additional indication of financial health. Substantial indebtedness to outside sources or even to other funds of the institution relative to the indebtedness that occurs in the normal course of doing business (current accounts payable and accrued taxes) are not strong positive signs of health.

As one measure of the weight of the burden of current indebtedness, we calculated the amount of current fund indebtedness on a full-time equivalent student basis, focusing our attention on the median institution in each of these groups.

The most striking fact is the very substantial indebtedness of $485 per student in Smallest institutions, for these are institutions with very substantial percentages of that indebtedness indicating longer term debt as over against that which is owed in the flow of current business. Over three-quarters of their current fund indebtedness is to private notes payable (other than current accounts payable and accrued taxes) and to other funds of the institution. At 8 percent interest that would amount to $24 per student annually. Small institutions, with 70 percent of their indebtedness to these same sources, also have a relatively substantial indebtedness per student of $295. The Medium group has a per student indebtedness of $205; for the Large group it is $175; and for the Largest group it is $185. The combined percentages of indebtedness to the two sources are, respectively 54, 59, and 46 percent.

There is not a great deal to distinguish one degree level group from another in dollar amounts per student except that the Doctor's group is relatively high at $370. Here, however, only 43 percent is to private notes payable and other funds of the institution combined. Bachelor's institutions and Limited Doctor's institutions have virtually identical dollar figures ($235 and $240 respectively), but $145 of the former's current fund indebtedness and only $60 of the latter's is to these two longer term indebtedness sources. Limited Master's institutions have a per student figure of $205 and Master's institutions have a figure of $220. Slightly over 50 percent of the indebtedness of both groups is to these two sources.

Direct Student Aid

The current fund account contains a subaccount that is called student aid, direct student aid, that is. Those who advise colleges in such matters recommend that the account include expenditures from both unrestricted and restricted current funds and that it include aid in the form of remitted tuition, except for remissions due to staff status. It should not include appropriations from governments to be loaned to students.

It does not always work that way. Some institutions take a short cut on the operation which underplays the amount of the institution's own money going into student aid. If an institution remits some or all of a student's tuition it may, on the grounds that no real money came in and no real money went out, simply record reduced revenue to the institution by indicating less income from tuition and fees in the educational and general subaccount. Unless the full amount of the tuition revenue due from that student is entered in educational and general, however, and the amount of tuition remission granted the student is entered as an expenditure in the student aid account, the extent of institutional subvention of student aid will be masked.

The amount of money expended on student aid in 1968, by the private colleges and universities of the nation taken as a whole, was equal to over 9 percent of educational and general expenditures; and slightly over 7 percent of the total current fund expenditures budget. This was equal to one-fourth of the total amount spent on instruction and departmental research; it was larger than the amount spent on physical plant operation and maintenance, and was nearly two and one-half times the amount spent on libraries.

In three years following 1968, student aid expenditures increased slightly their portion of the total current fund expenditures, grew at a slightly faster rate than educational and general, and picked up an additional five percentage points on the amount spent on libraries. The amount spent on instruction and departmental research, however, increased at a slightly faster rate than student aid.

In 1968 the average amount expended per student on direct student aid in the group of Large institutions was $220, and this was the lowest amount spent by any enrollment group. The pattern, thereafter, followed that of the educational and general (less sponsored research and medical center expenditures) cost per student analysis (see Table 20). In both 1968 and 1969 the lower the average cost per student, the lower the average expenditure on direct student aid. The group providing the next lowest average direct student aid in 1968 was, therefore, the Small. Third lowest was the Medium. Fourth and fifth places were taken by, respectively, the Smallest and the Largest.

By degree levels, there is not a very noticeable difference in the average amount of direct student aid offered between Bachelor's institutions and Limited Master's institutions. In general, however, the more complex the institution, the greater the amount of direct student aid offered. The nature and extent of the graduate programs offered by a group of institutions clearly influences the amount of direct student aid which that group expends. The ranking of the degree level groups by average direct student aid per student parallels (as does the enrollment group ranking) the educational and general cost per student with one exception. Whereas the lowest educational and general cost per student is at the Bachelor's institution and the other groups follow in order of increasing complexity, the Bachelor's institution does not have a lower average

Table 27. DIRECT STUDENT AID PER STUDENT FOR 1968 AND 1969

	1968	1969	Increase
Institutions by Enrollment Groups			
Smallest	$244	$248	$24
Small	195	227	32
Medium	216	245	29
Large	196	220	24
Largest	318	351	33
Institutions by Degree Levels			
Bachelor's	$185	$212	$27
Limited Master's	185	208	23
Master's	202	232	30
Limited Doctor's	265	296	31
Doctor's	402	442	40

in direct student aid than Limited Master's institutions. (See Table 27.)

Another measure of the amount of student aid being expended through the current fund of the private institutions may be seen when this amount is compared with the income derived from tuition and fees. Nationally for the years embraced by these data, student aid has equalled approximately 18 percent of tuition and fee income, rising from 17.6 to 18.2 then to 18.3 and then down to 18.1. The median, however, has run just under 14 percent. One quarter of the institutions provide direct student aid that is 9.5 percent or less of their tuition and fee income; one quarter provide aid that is 23 percent or more of that income. There are exceptional institutions with a combination of low tuition and high student aid that can boast of spending an amount on total student aid that is equal to 150 percent of their reported tuition and fee income. There are also one or two institutions reporting no direct student aid, possibly because the indirect student aid for all students is as high as it is.

These paragraphs set the stage for making three points. The first is that a very large and increasing amount of money is being spent on direct student aid. This is a considerable burden on private higher education and a very important factor in its deficit condition.

The second point is that private higher education is caught in an ever widening and more vicious cycle. As it moves to demonstrate its social concern by extending scholarship money to those unable to pay even the costs of education assigned to them through tuition, it must find revenue to pay for these student aid expenditures. Typically it has done this, in large part, by raising tuition. In doing so, however, it puts the full tuition charge to the students out of reach for another group of students, who now require subsidy for the difference between last year's cost and this year's. This, in turn, requires further tuition increases, creates still another group needing financial aid, increases the amount of aid needed by the groups previously identified, and so on.

The third point is that a certain amount of accounting artificiality is connected with student aid on the income side which results in large deficits in this category. A large deficit shows up in this account because the institution assigns little income to offset these expenditures. There is, to be sure, typically very little institutional income specifically related to student aid. But then, the same thing could be said about many items found under educational and general expenditures. General administration, student services, and general institutional expenses, for example, are not attached to educational and general income by any inherent necessity. Theoretically, at least, one could put student aid in their place, run a bigger surplus in education and general, and a bigger deficit in the new account created for general administration, student services, and general institutional expenses.

Partly because of the way in which certain revenues are balanced against certain other expenditures, but even more because of the rising dollar share of direct student aid, the total current fund deficit for many institutions very nearly equals the deficit in the subaccount for student aid. The total current fund deficit seems to be growing even faster than the student aid deficit, but there is a high degree of correlation between them. Many a private institution now running a current fund deficit would break even if its direct student aid deficit were lifted from its back.

The way in which accountants package higher education accounts ought not be a barrier to the consideration of a variety of types of state and federal aid. It is apparent that aid that would reduce the burden of an institution's commitment to further subsidize its own students would be welcome and helpful. It is not the only form that aid can take, however, to be helpful to the total operation of the institution.

If a swimmer could carry a one hundred pound burden across a river but is given two bundles, one weighing ninety pounds and the other thirty, he will drown. It is idle to ask which bundle caused him to drown. If it is easier to relieve him of one bundle than another, this ought to be done. If the contents of the bundles are to some extent interchangeable, however, there may be more than one way to relieve him sufficiently to enable him to make his way across.

Indirect Student Aid

In addition to direct student aid (the amount of money an institution makes available to students to help them defray *their* cost of education), there is an indirect student aid which is the difference

between the amount charged to the student (whether or not defrayed
for him by direct student aid) and what it actually costs the institu-
ion to provide the student with his education. Indirect student aid
is the financial gap between tuition and actual instructional costs.
The gap exists in all higher education except for that provided
under proprietary auspices. It is greatest in public higher education
where tuition is low or nonexistent; but it exists in very substantial
amounts in private higher education as well.

The struggling student or his suffering parent, confronted
with large tuition charges and other expenses concomitant with
securing a higher education, may be forgiven for having only a dim
awareness that the full cost for the services the student is receiving
is not covered by the tuition and fees paid. It may be useful, however, to sharpen that awareness.

The category Tuition and Fees is probably self-explanatory.
This is the income received from the student which ostensibly covers
the cost of instruction together with special charges for such things
as laboratory breakage fees. Cost of instruction is defined as all
expenditures normally listed as educational and general expenses
(but not the cost of sponsored research and the expenses involved
in a medical center). This cost of instruction would therefore include faculty compensation (salaries and fringe benefits); library
costs; the operation and maintenance of the physical plant; student
services (counseling, placement, and the like); and general administration expenses. It would not include capital costs, residence hall
costs, dining services, or direct student aid costs.

Mark Hopkins and his log still make up the lion's share of
this cost of instruction but it now includes Mark's retirement fund,
a room to house the log and someone to keep it dusted, as well as
someone to record who sat on the log how long and with what
results.

Indirect student aid is greatest on a per student basis at the
very smallest and the very largest institutions. Smallest institutions
are subsidizing their students' education more highly than any other
enrollment group. At over 1000 dollars per student ($1053) their
indirect student aid is 35 percent more than that of Largest institutions ($782), 68 percent more than of Small institutions ($627),

and over twice as much as of Medium institutions ($507) and
Large ($475).

Since indirect student subsidy is a function of the instructional cost per student and the percentage that tuition and fee income is to the cost of instruction, the very smallest institutions, with
a high cost per student and the lowest percentage contribution toward the cost of instruction from tuition and fee income, have the
highest indirect student aid per student. The Largest institutions
have a higher cost per student but derive a larger percentage of
instructional expenditures from tuition income and therefore provide a smaller indirect student aid per student. Large institutions
have the second lowest cost per student of all the enrollment groups,
derive the highest percentage of instructional costs from tuition income, and provide the lowest indirect student aid subsidy.

By degree level groupings, the largest indirect student aid is
provided by Doctor's institutions. This is two and one-half times as
much as that provided by non-Doctoral institutions and nearly twice
as much as that provided by Limited Doctor's institutions. Reflect-
ing both the high instructional costs of graduate programs and the
relatively small amount of those costs recovered through tuition,
Doctor's institutions provide an average indirect student aid subsidy of $1119 per student. Limited Doctor's institutions provide
$572. Bachelor's institutions are third with an indirect student aid
subsidy of $466. Then come Limited Master's institutions ($431)
followed by Master's institutions ($412).

Indirect student aid varies considerably between one geographical region and another but with no patently discernible
relationship to the overall financial well being of the colleges and
universities in that region. It is as low as $435 in the Mountain
Region and as high as $950 per student in the New England Re-
gion. Two other regions are in the $400's (Mid-Atlantic, $448,
and East North Central, $490), and two are in the $800's (South
Atlantic, $863, and West North Central, $821). The remaining
three are in between: Pacific ($608), West South Central ($592),
East South Central ($727). This proves to be the mid-point for
the nation as a whole. For all private colleges and universities in
the study the annual indirect student aid per student is $638. This
substantial amount of pocket money must be taken into account

whenever such issues as social/individual benefits from higher education vis à vis social/individual contributions toward the cost of that education are totaled up. All students in post-secondary higher education—except those in proprietory schools—are recipients of the benefactions of others. Indirect student aid constitutes an important subvention of their education by concerned members of the public.

The amount of indirect student aid provided by an institution depends upon the cost of instruction at that institution as well as the percentage that tuition is of educational and general income. The great disparity in amounts between, say, complex graduate institutions and baccalaureate institutions influences the disparity evident in comparisons of relatively small subsamples of institutions, depending upon the mix of institutions involved. Among regions, for example, the low dollar amount of indirect student aid per student in the Mountain Region is a factor of the relatively small size of the baccalaureate institutions in the region rather than any factor of geography.

Great differences in indirect aid can also be identified when the groupings are states or denominations. North Carolina, with sixteen institutions reporting, has an indirect student aid figure of $131. Missouri, with seventeen institutions reporting, has an indirect student aid figure of $1928. Among religious groups the range is from $192 for the Quaker related institutions and $211 for those related to the Church of the Nazarene, to $766 for Seventh Day Adventist colleges, $908 for those independent of church relationship, and $1252 for those related to the Episcopal Church. There is no consistent relationship between the amount of dollar support from the denomination and the per student dollar amount of indirect student aid. The Seventh Day Adventists and the Church of the Nazarene are first and second in support for their colleges in terms of percent of current fund expenditures; the Episcopal Church is second to the last in its support to its colleges. Yet, as seen by the figures above, the colleges related to the Episcopal Church have the highest indirect student aid, followed by Independent and Seventh Day Adventist colleges; while the Church of the Nazarene colleges, second highest in support received from the denomination, are second lowest in the amount of indirect student aid.

Review of Expenditure Problems

Some of the influences on the rate of expenditure are beyond the college's control. Inflation, for example, like the mischievous thumb of the butcher, has exerted a continual, if uneven pressure on the scales that measure the goods and services which colleges must purchase. This influence is not new to this decade or this century. According to Seymour Harris, with the single exception of the first quarter of the nineteenth century, every financial crisis in our oldest institution's history came in periods of inflation.[2] The return to an inflationary rate nearer 3 percent offers a somewhat brighter outlook than the 4 to 6 percent rates of the late sixties, although some of the goods and services purchased by colleges and universities are likely to continue inflating at rates higher than these.

Some expenditure items are relatively new for many institutions. The computer presents one such set of new costs. As an instrument for research and teaching the computer expands the capacity of the institution to serve in those two ways. Yet it does not replace less expensive methods, and its use means increased costs, not cost savings. When computers are used in the administration of colleges and universities they may be of aid in reducing costs. Smaller institutions, however, would be wise to proceed cautiously in this area. The lure of a computer-organized management information system as a device to ensure more efficient management probably should be resisted in most smaller private colleges until a competent cost benefit analysis of the computer's operation has been performed. Thus far it has not been demonstrated that the benefits of a sophisticated computer system are not outweighed by the costs of obtaining those benefits. At this stage, the calculator, combined with realistic planning and better accounting methods, offers a surer return on their investment to most small institutions.

Another brand new cost for many institutions, Jenny and

2 Seymour E. Harris, "Financing Higher Education: An Overview," in *The Economics and Financing of Higher Education in the United States* (Washington, D.C.: Government Printing Office, 1969), p. 468.

Wynn have reminded us, is debt service.[3] Construction expenditures, swelled by high rates of inflation in the construction industry, increased during the early sixties at an average annual rate of 19.7 percent. Revenue for capital improvement purposes increased at the lower rate of 16.9 percent. As the decade proceeded, moreover, loans constituted an increasingly larger share of those revenues, growing from one-third to one-half. This fact, coupled with rising rates on borrowing, put the average private institution into indebtedness on its physical plant equal to one-quarter of the book value of the plant. Principal repayments plus interest, carried in the current account, increased from fifty-nine dollars per student in 1966 (according to a study of independent colleges in Pennsylvania) to eighty-eight dollars per student five years later.

What is disturbing about this expenditure item is not merely its newness or its magnitude but the hint it provides of future financial stress. The buildings constructed in the sixties must not only be maintained, they must one day be renovated and, ultimately, replaced. The spectre of a severe financial threat lurks behind these future plant needs. Jenny and Wynn have estimated that the forty-eight liberal arts colleges they studied will have capital requirements in excess of one billion dollars before the end of this century. Whether these institutions move to set up adequate reserves now (which is Jenny and Wynn's[4] and this author's recommendation) or borrow for renovation and replacement when the need arises, another fixed cost of substantial dimensions will be added to future budgets. Anyone who imagines that private colleges have turned the financial corner by a temporary curtailment of expenditures has not sufficiently contemplated the renovation and replacement costs that lie ahead.

Among the expanded services which private colleges and universities have been providing their several constituencies, none has had a more subtly distending effect on college expenditures than that agglomeration of expenses known as student services. These have been added to the college's operation in much the same way a New England farmhouse is put together. New services have

[3] Jenny and Wynn, *The Golden Years*, p. 57.
[4] Jenny and Wynn, *The Turning Point*, p. 54.

been added or enlarged as new needs—real or supposed—have appeared.

The range of student services, which many colleges provide in response to putative student needs, is virtually wall to wall. These include counseling—psychological, academic, and personal (sometimes including family problems); long- and short-term medical treatment; placement services; and still other programs. The problem is not only that these services have not been subjected to very sophisticated cost analyses, as G. Wayne Glick has pointed out,[5] but that analysis of the benefit derived from offering these services is even further behind. While working toward the identification of the true cost—and benefit—of these institutionalized services, a college needs to reconsider which of the services it has been beguiled into providing are essential to its operation as an academic institution and deserving of subsidization from general funds, and which might be offered to the student either from other suppliers or for additional fees. More efficient restructuring of student services is needed.

Faculty compensation climbed steadily during the sixties at a rate higher than inflation; salaries were increased not only because of market conditions and organized pressure, but also because there was common agreement that faculty members were underpaid vis à vis other vocational segments of society. In some institutions they appear still badly underpaid in proportion to the significance of their contribution to society. In all institutions they appear underpaid in comparison to the outrageously disproportionate reward tendered some other segments of society.

The time has come, however, to ask if faculty salaries in many institutions may not have achieved some reasonable balance in relation to most other professional segments of the population. Since there is no grand arbiter to set parity for faculty compensation, the market and other pressures will move to create one. It would be regrettable if the contemporary abundance of potential faculty members in the market prompted a relapse in the gains made in the last decade; but it is unrealistic to believe that the financial condi-

[5] G. Wayne Glick, "Student Services," in William W. Jellema, ed., *Efficient College Management* (San Francisco: Jossey-Bass, 1972), p. 101.

tion of private institutions will permit further gains on the rest of
the population of this same magnitude. Increases in faculty compensation that more nearly approximate the rate of inflation may
represent equity for the next decade.

V

Responses to
Deficits

What happens when more goes out than comes in? When a college gets to the end of its budget and still has a lot of calendar left? We asked the colleges that reported a deficit in 1968 what they had done to meet that deficit. The options offered to this question were those that had monetary implications. Tearing one's hair out, weeping on the shoulders of peers, or repenting in sackcloth and ashes, while perhaps offering psychological catharsis, do not produce fiscal solutions to fiscal problems.

In order of frequency the options checked were: borrow—other (including from current funds); transfer from unappropriated surplus; raise tuition; increase fund-raising activities, defer maintenance, retrench expenditures, transfer from other reserves, borrow—from endowment, spend principal of funds functioning as endowment, cut back on depreciation allowance, spend appreciation on endowment funds.

The most popular responses—"borrow—other (including from current funds)" and "transfer from unappropriated surplus" —were conditioned, of course, by the availability of loan money and the rate at which it was available, as well as by the presence or absence of unappropriated surplus. An institution with no unappropriated surplus did not have the option of using it to cover its deficit, even as an institution without credit standing could not borrow. Both types seem to exist. There are a large number of institutions without any "unappropriated surplus," and one hears rumors that there are others unable to borrow money.

To the option "borrow—other" we specifically added the words "including from current funds" because the pilot run of the questionnaire uncovered a curious maneuver; curious, not meaning suspect in a business sense, but curious in an accounting sense.

We encountered an institution which reported a deficit but which chose none of the options from our supposedly inclusive list to explain what it was doing about it. (At that time the option read, simply, "borrow—other" to distinguish from "borrow—from endowment.") When the institution was asked to explain, the chief business officer said simply, "I'm not doing anything about it. I'm simply covering it with the flow of money." What he meant was that he was covering a current (or past) deficit by using the advance payment of monies (tuition) paid for services yet to be rendered.

Two or three things need to be said about this maneuver. The first is that this is not an unfamiliar practice in business. The cash flow is not infrequently or inappropriately used to cover an operating deficit. This is an interest-free way of handling a short-term liquidity problem.

It is, however, an act of borrowing and should be so noted in order to present an accurate picture of the financial state of the institution. It is, in fact, a borrowing from current funds. (See Chapter One.) Moreover, it is a little like putting a larger fuse in the fuse box if smaller sizes keep getting blown: it masks the fact that there is a problem which needs correction before it becomes a bigger problem, and thus it eliminates an early danger signal. Cash flow does have some elasticity and can be used to stretch a bridge across a temporary chasm; but it is not infinitely elastic. It is dangerous to believe that one need do "nothing" about a deficit.

There is no guarantee, of course, that simply adding the words "including from current funds" to the first option made this point clear to other institutions engaged in the same operation. Indeed, there is some evidence to suggest that it did not.

Part of that evidence may be contained in further responses to this same question. The third most frequent answer to the question "How did you meet your deficit?" was "raise tuition." This may or may not be an accurate perception of the question. Since the respondents were not limited to a single answer and the responses are not additive, it may be that these colleges are saying that, in addition to taking some immediate action such as borrowing, they raised tuition as a means of paying back that loan, and, perhaps, of avoiding a deficit the following year. It may also be true that some of those checking this option are saying that they were able to receive a loan on the basis of the expected income to be created by the tuition increase.

But in those few cases where a deficit was recorded and the only option checked was "raise tuition," one is entitled to the strong suspicion that money was borrowed from current funds and the "No action necessary, I am covering with cash flow" gambit is being employed.

Similar assumptions can be made from several other options including the next most popular for 1968: "Increase fund raising activities." Here, of course, there is less likelihood than in the case of tuition that any institution secured a loan on the basis of the promise of increased activities in this area. When an institution selected this option to describe its response to a deficit, it may have been describing a secondary decision about what it planned to do in the future rather than submitting an accurate answer about how it actually met a deficit. Again, in those cases where a deficit was recorded and this was the only option checked, something slipped either in a conceptual or in an accounting sense.

A different picture appears when one examines the responses to the question, "If you did not report a deficit, did you avoid a deficit by action in any of (these) areas . . . ?" An institution that can project an anticipated deficit far enough in advance has somewhat broader options than has the institution taken by surprise.

Not unexpectedly, and legitimately (in the sense of being accurate both in conceptual and in an accounting sense) "raise tuition" leads as an answer to this question. Nearly twice as many respondents indicated that they raised tuition over any other option. Tuition and fee increases, although turned to reluctantly by private colleges and universities, have been the most flexible and immediate source of increased income.

All of these responses are ground for some concern, some more so than others. One that especially caught our attention was "borrowing—from endowment."

It is called "borrowing" instead of "spending"—which it is —because the institution hopes to pay it back. Although this was the last thing large institutions reported doing, it was frequently noted by small baccalaureate institutions.

Primers on college accounting identify three principal kinds of endowment all of which may be classified according to limitations placed upon the use of income derived from them. There are, first of all, true endowment funds. These are monies given to an institution with the stipulation that the principal be kept inviolate in perpetuity and only the income expended. Then there are term endowment funds. These are given with the understanding that after a specified period, the principal no longer must be kept inviolate and may be expended. Finally, there are quasi-endowment funds or funds functioning as endowment. These are funds that the governing board has decided to retain and invest. In general, principal as well as income may be expended by that same board at any time. These funds may be either unrestricted in the uses of income derived from investment, restricted in use, or designated. The last is a board determination as distinct from a donor designation.

The distinction between unrestricted endowment (inviolate principal but without limitations on uses of income) and funds functioning as endowment (invested at the discretion of the board and whose principal may be expended if the board so determines) is not a distinction well understood by all of the respondents, as we discovered. An institution is, of course, legally free to use its funds functioning as endowment if this proves necessary. When an institution spends the principal of those funds, however, it not only loses those funds but also loses the dividend income and appreciation on those funds which it had probably been using for current operations. It must then find money to make up this loss both in the year in which it spends the principal and in the years that follow. An institution may borrow from its funds functioning as endowment for purposes that carry the institution a major step forward. If the borrowing is done simply to keep the institution operating, however, this is clearly a danger signal to the institution and to those concerned about the future of higher education.

We were especially concerned to note that some institutions were borrowing principal from unrestricted endowment funds. Curiously, the law regarding endowment funds is in its infancy; there is very little precedent in the courts on endowment. What there is stems from state court decisions in which endowment is generally treated in one of three ways: educational institutions are held to be the absolute owners of the endowment funds, or they are viewed as holding their endowment in trust for their students or for society, or they may be viewed as trustees of their own endowment funds.

Nonetheless, borrowing from endowment principal seems very questionable both ethically and legally in most states, unless the donor specifically permitted the use of principal as well as income in the event of financial exigency. Should an institution be forced to close its doors, the doctrine of *cy pres* would seem to require that the donor's intention in giving the gift of endowment be permitted to continue, perhaps in some similar institution. How can this be done if the endowment has been hypothecated? Who is responsible if endowment has been offered and accepted as security for a loan whose payment cannot be fulfilled? These are awkward questions for any institution actually hypothecating endowment principal.

To try to find out the magnitude of this practice we asked specifically, "Has your institution borrowed from unrestricted endowment principal?" To our surprise, one-fourth of the institutions in the study—including institutions in every enrollment group and degree level category—reported that they had so borrowed, and that their borrowing amounted to 24 percent of the market value of their unrestricted endowment. In some geographical regions the percentage of institutions reporting borrowing was heavier than in others: 36 percent in Pacific, 33 percent in West and East North Central, 25 percent in Mountain, 22 percent in East South Central, 16 to 18 percent along the Atlantic coast and West South Central. (These percentages would be higher if they were limited to the number of institutions in the region that reported having unrestricted endowment.) The percentage of those reporting borrowing was especially high in some states: 50 percent in Minnesota, 45 percent in Ohio and Illinois, 44 percent in Washington, 36 percent in California. Borrowers tended to be roughly equally distributed among the degree level groups with the percentage of borrowers running from 24 percent among the Bachelor's institutions to 28 percent among the Doctor's institutions. The exception was the group of Limited Doctor's institutions; only 10 percent of these reported borrowing.

Not all of these institutions were as precise in their responses as our question intended. In further communication with them we discerned that one-third meant that they had borrowed from funds functioning as endowment, not from unrestricted endowment. The remaining 67 percent, however, meant what they said. Invasion of endowment by a quarter of private institutions is a significant fact —even if the endowment is quasi-endowment rather than unrestricted endowment in some cases.

Seventy-two percent of this borrowing was for plant, 26 percent went into the current fund, and 2 percent was described as committed otherwise. There is some difference of opinion on the wisdom of investing endowment principal in institutional property. Most advise against it, but some feel the practice is legitimate if the property is income-producing, such as residence halls. (The trouble is, they may not always be income producing.) On the question of borrowing against unrestricted endowment principal for current operations, however, there is little disagreement: the practice should not be countenanced.

Another practice whose legal appropriateness is sometimes questioned (when it concerns true endowment funds and not quasi-endowment funds) is the practice of adding realized capital gains on investment to dividend return and applying some portion of this total return (or total yield) to the support of the operating budget. Legal opinion varies from one state to another. The issue centers on whether or not the growth of the investment may be considered part of the return or must be considered part of the principal.

Whether applied to true endowment or quasi-endowment the concept is a relatively new one which was described in the Ford Foundation's *Managing Educational Endowments* published originally in 1969 and further advanced by John F. Meck of Dartmouth among others.[1]

To find out how extensive this practice had become we asked: "Do you regularly assign some portion of realized capital gains of your endowment to the support of the operating budget?" One-eighth responded in the affirmative. The percentages tended to be higher in the West North Central region (20 percent), the West South Central region (18 percent), and the Pacific region (15 percent); and lower in the New England and East South Central region (9 percent). The percentage runs as high as 25 in Kansas and Minnesota, 21 in Iowa, 17 in New York and Illinois. We asked the question, incidentally, at that moment in recent history (May, 1970) when a sustained bear market had just reached its greatest intensity. It will be interesting to repeat the question in a few years to see whether its acceptance is growing.

We also tried to find out what portion of realized capital gains expressed as a dollar amount or as a percentage of accretion most institutions were taking. A little less than half indicated that they had determined a specific dollar amount that they assigned to the operating budget taken as realized capital gains from endowment. The remainder worked from a variety of percentage formulas. About one-eighth of these take it all; 100 percent of the capital gains realized are applied to the operating budget. Most of the remainder used some percentage as their yardstick, frequently 5 percent of the market value of the endowment. Most of these set this as a rate of expected return from the endowment and took as

[1] *Managing Educational Endowments: Report to the Ford Foundation* (2nd ed.) (New York, 1972).

realized capital gains whatever was necessary as a supplement to cash dividends and interest to reach this rate. At its most sophisticated, this was stated as 5 percent of the three-year average value of the investment portfolio.

Federal Aid

The essence of overcoming deficits is either to reduce expenditures or seek additional income. The latter is by far the preferred alternative. Almost everyone's preferred source of aid—and not just everyone in higher education—is the federal government. The federal government has the taxing strength and therefore the revenue that smaller units of government do not have and is presumed to be less idiosyncratic in its judgments than local offices. Moreover, every problem, as seen from the perspective of those wrestling with it, is a national problem. Basically, however, it is the potfuls of money the federal government has or, so some believed, would have when the Vietnam enterprise ended, that drew the attention of the importunate.

The federal government's annual expenditure in education is estimated by the Federal Interagency Committee on Education to be fourteen billion dollars. How much of that was finding its way into the operation of the private nonprofit four-year colleges and universities of the land and in what form? Responding institutions were asked how much federal money they received in any one year for capital funds (both buildings and equipment) and for current funds (including research, teaching improvement, student aid, libraries, etc.). We asked for the amount of the expended dollar, not, for example, the amount of money awarded in one year but to be spent over a period of years.

Responses from 488 institutions totalled 606 million dollars in 1968, 703 million in 1969 (a 16 percent increase), and 587 million in 1970 (a 16.5 percent decrease). There appear to be gaps in these responses. It is difficult for a small institution to keep track of all federal monies it receives and it is a complex problem for a large institution to account for its federal funds under these categories. These totals therefore probably understate the true totals. Nevertheless, if the federal government is spending the bulk of its fourteen billion educational dollars in any one place, that place does not appear to be private higher education.

The bulk of the service rendered for those federal funds has been research. In 1969 research money constituted nearly half (48.4 percent) of all the federal monies reported by the institution in the study. However, only 41 percent of the private institutions reported sharing in this largess. Half of the total federal dollar received by private institutions, in other words, went to less than half of the institutions. In fact, 92 percent of the research money went to Ph.D. granting institutions. In the years before and after 1969, research constituted a smaller percentage of the total federal dollar —44.2 percent in both years. However, the percentage of institutions sharing this research dollar did not change.

In 1968 the second largest amount (19.2 percent) of federal grants received by private colleges and universities went for buildings. Third place went to student aid at 17.7 percent. In 1969 student aid edged out buildings (which had declined to 16.1 percent) and claimed a secure hold on it in 1970 when its percentage rose to 21.1 percent, while buildings held constant at 16.2 percent. There is this further difference: the money for buildings has gone, in any given year, to no more than 38 percent of the institutions, while 85 percent had student aid money to report.

Money for teaching improvement programs is the only other large category of federal funds that these institutions reported receiving. Approximately 10 percent of the federal money goes into programs of this nature at about 40 percent of the institutions. Small percentages are received for equipment (2.5, 1.7, 1.6 for each of the three years) and for miscellaneous (6.6, 6.8, 6.0 percent), of which perhaps 0.3 percent was identifiable as being for libraries.

It is striking to contrast the different kinds of aid which the enrollment and degree level groups receive. The fact that 55.1 percent of the federal aid that Smallest institutions receive is for buildings and 0.7 percent for research is eloquent testimony to the style of their kind of education. It is not hard to see why they prefer federal support for brick and mortar and are utterly unenthusiastic for research support. The percentage distributions for Small institutions is much the same: substantially for buildings and student aid.

The group of Largest institutions has a pattern of support that is quite different; the federal research dollar accounts for 56.3 percent of the federal income of these institutions, with only 10.5 percent for buildings and 13 percent for student aid.

The same data analyzed by degree levels show the expected decline in the significance of federal money received for construction: 30 percent of the money that Bachelor's institutions receive from the federal government is for this purpose, less than 9 percent at Doctor's institutions. Research money shows a different pattern. For all of the groups less complex than Doctor's institutions, approximately 36 percent is received for research. Limited Master's institutions are an exception. A much larger percentage of what this group receives comes under the category of student aid or miscellaneous than is true for the other groups. The Doctor's institutions have the expected high percentage for research (60 percent) and the concomitant low percentages for buildings (8.7 percent) and for student aid (11.5 percent). These figures are given in Table 28.

These figures, of course, offer little or no commentary upon the relative amounts of money which these various groups of institutions receive, what the relation to their need might be, or what a proper share of the federal dollar would be. All that these percentages show is how what they in fact receive is distributed among various programs of federal support. We can come a little closer to the more substantive questions by some of the data which follow.

We sought to discover what these dollar figures and percentages might mean if translated into dollars per full-time equivalent student. The sampling was limited to the number of institutions reporting receipt of federal funds in a given category. For example, the number of institutions that report in a given year—say, 1969— receipt of money for equipment is only 45 percent of the total. The number reporting receipt of money for buildings is 38 percent. The remaining institutions may well have received money for these purposes in either the previous or succeeding year. Nonetheless, in some smaller sub-groups the sample size is reduced considerably. These data probably point in the right direction without having the same accuracy that a moving picture and larger sample sizes would provide.

Equipment and buildings were merged as a single capital

Table 28. PERCENTAGE DISTRIBUTION OF FEDERAL FUNDS RECEIVED: 1969

	Equipment	Buildings	Research	Teaching Improvement	Student Aid	Miscellaneous	Total[b]
Enrollment Groups							
Smallest	1.2	55.1	0.7	6.6	32.4	4.1	100.1
Small	2.2	50.2	3.8	5.1	33.0	5.6	99.9
Medium[a]	2.2	38.9	5.9	5.4	39.9	7.7	100.0
Large	4.0	28.1	25.6	4.4	24.6	13.3	100.0
Largest	1.6	10.5	56.3	12.1	13.0	6.5	100.0
Degree Levels							
Bachelor's	1.6	30.1	36.0	3.9	25.1	3.3	100.0
Limited Master's	2.3	29.6	9.5	8.1	37.5	13.1	100.1
Master's	5.6	20.1	36.9	5.1	25.6	6.7	100.0
Limited Doctor's	1.1	18.9	35.8	14.7	18.1	11.4	100.0
Doctor's	1.4	8.7	60.0	11.8	11.5	6.5	99.9

[a] 1970 figures used for this group.
[b] Totals may not equal 100.0 per cent because of rounding.

funds category and the remaining current fund items appear under another single category. Examined by enrollment groups, these data suggest that Smallest institutions do not fare nearly as well as the other groups. Their current fund figure of twenty-six dollars per student compares very favorably with all save the group of Largest institutions; but the thirty-one dollars per student for capital funds is so much less than other groups that the total per student dollar is only slightly more than half the next lowest group, the Large. The Medium group fares best on the capital funds dollar; but the Largest group fares best on the total.

Analyzed by degree levels, Bachelor's institutions receive the least amount of money per student for current fund items collectively of any degree level group. However, differences among Bachelor's and the three other groups pale into insignificance alongside the funds that Doctor's institutions receive, twenty-five to forty-seven times larger than those of any other group.

In terms of capital funds, Bachelor's institutions do not fare badly. They run a close third place after the two groups offering the doctorate. In total dollars, the Masters does least well. These comparisons are set forth in Table 29.

Based on this experience each college president was asked to

Table 29. FEDERAL MONEY RECEIVED PER FULL-TIME EQUIVALENT STUDENT AT THE MEDIAN INSTITUTION: 1969

	Current Funds	Capital Funds	Total
Enrollment Group			
Smallest	$ 26	$ 31	$ 57
Small	12	125	137
Medium	16	149	165
Large	33	77	110
Largest	110	82	192
Degree Level			
Bachelor's	$ 18	$ 85	$103
Limited Master's	33	31	64
Master's	23	37	60
Limited Doctor's	30	92	122
Doctor's	853	96	949

indicate the types of federal aid he favored as part of a balanced program. He had three basic options. He could indicate which ones he preferred; he could indicate which ones he found acceptable even if he did not prefer them; or he could indicate that certain types were unacceptable to him. In addition, of course, he could indicate that he preferred no form of federal aid, although in fact nobody did so. The president could also identify some form of federal aid other than the eleven basic types we had listed, and 61 presidents did so, coming up with an interesting and often imaginative array of other options. He could, finally, simply by-pass a decision on any one or all of the types we presented to him.

The type of federal aid which was most often checked as "preferred" was: facilities grants directly to institutions. This was an option familiar to most respondents. They have tried it. They like it and they want more of it. This was, in the most precise sense of the word, a conservative choice.

The next preferred type of federal aid was: institutional grants directly to institutions. This was not a conservative choice in the sense of being based upon experience with federal aid. It bears, however, an apparent resemblance to other monies that come to an institution to be used at its discretion and doubtless seemed a conservative choice, and should be interpreted as being a simple and straightforward endorsement of a form of aid which appears unentangling. The question was not sufficiently refined to reveal, however, what formula for the assignment of this aid would be acceptable or (and this applies with equal force to many other options) what kinds of "strings" (if any) would make federal aid in this form acceptable and what kinds would make it unwelcome.

The next most frequently preferred choice was: grants directly to students. This is, again, a type of federal aid with which colleges and universities have had a lot of experience. Most of that experience, to judge by this response, has been good. Aid has been too meager and too inconstant, but it has demonstrated its value and is a popular choice.

Facilities loans (as distinct from facilities grants) directly to institutions was identified fourth most often as a preferred choice.

The type of federal aid fifth most frequently identified as preferred was: a federally supported student loan bank. This is not a conservative choice in the sense of being based on experience. It is an idea recently endorsed by the Carnegie Commission on Higher Education and many individual economists as part of a balanced program of federal aid. It would, in essence, make available at low interest federally guaranteed loan funds that could be borrowed by individual students to cover their educational costs (including but not limited to tuition) and repaid by them at a rate proportionate to later income.

In sixth place on the preferred list was: other loans directly to students.

Next most frequently chosen was a proposal which has been around a long time: income tax credit for student expenditures. Many of its proponents are very clear and sometimes single-minded in their espousal of this form of aid. It has, however, a small group of opponents who may feel that not enough is known of its economic effects.

Two choices tied for eighth place: interest subsidy and categorical grants to institutions for research and programs. In tenth place: grants to the states for distribution to institutions; and eleventh: grants to the states for distribution to students.

When preferred types of federal aid are added with acceptable types, however, some interesting things happen.

Facilities grants directly to institutions remains in first place, being identified 516 times (out of 549) as either preferred or acceptable. Immediately behind it, however, run five other options, separated from one another by a total spread of only eleven votes. These are other loans directly to students (505), federally supported student loan bank (504), facilities loans directly to institutions (499), institutional grants directly to institutions (498), grants directly to students (494). This may suggest that private institutions are so anxious for federal aid that virtually any form could be at least acceptable even if some forms of it appear preferable. One respondent may have been speaking for others when he added: "Anything to obtain more funds would at least be acceptable."

Even in a quick overview at least two other observations are striking. When acceptable are added to preferred, other loans directly to students moves from sixth to second place and federally supported student loan bank moves from fifth to third. This suggests that many institutions view student loans as a highly acceptable kind of federal aid although it may not give the institution the same freedom (and hence is not as preferred) as some forms of aid to the institution itself. The other observation is that income tax credit for student expenditures slips from seventh to ninth, falling behind even categorical grants to institutions for research and programs, and interest subsidy.

It is interesting to reorder the ranking in terms of unacceptability. Since most private institutions seem to indicate by their response that they could live happily with federal aid in almost any form, any type of aid that is judged unacceptable by a substantial number must be anathema indeed.

The aid that is most often judged unacceptable is that which would come either to institutions or to students by way of the states. (State-wide coordinating boards, who might be expected to take another view of this, were not included in the survey.) Twenty-eight percent of the presidents responding said that they would find unacceptable aid that came to the institution by way of a detour through the states and over 31 percent said that they would find unacceptable aid that came to the students in this round-about way.

It is curious, in a way, that private institutions are so wary of aid coming to them from the federal government by way of the states. Private institutions have an argument for preferential treatment going for them at the state level that is not as strong at the federal level. The appeal to the taxpayer is more direct and immediate. The private institution can argue forcibly at the state level that the taxpayer saves more money by subsidizing viable private institutions than by taking over responsibility for educating those students which private institutions enroll. The federal government, which has a less immediate relationship with any institution, public or private, is probably more open to persuasion by the more philosophical argument regarding the need for pluralism and diversity than it is by the economic argument. Private institutions have already discovered the success of this economic argument in many state legislatures.

Perhaps this negative judgment on federal aid via the states contains an implicit comment on revenue sharing; but it is more likely that it springs out of a mounting concern for the growing

power of state coordinating agencies. It does not seem to be related to whether or not the state in which an institution finds itself
has already acted with legislation favorable to private higher education. Thus, institutions in Illinois—which has a program of state
aid for students in private institutions—are more skeptical of federal
aid to students via the states than institutions in the state of Missouri
—which had none at the time the question was asked. There was a
higher percentage of negative attitude toward federal aid in either
of these two forms among institutions in the South and in New
England than elsewhere in the nation. Forty-seven percent of the
institutions in the East South Central region reported that aid to institutions in this fashion would be unacceptable, and 39 percent
reported negatively on aid to students. Fifty-six percent of the responding institutions in Maryland, burned by an unfavorable decision in that state's Court of Appeals in 1966, indicated that they
would find unacceptable federal aid to institutions that came by
way of the state. Larger institutions as well as Doctor's institutions
are more likely to find acceptable federal aid to either students or
institutions that comes by way of the states than are those institutions that are either small or less complex.

    Not enough study and planning has yet taken place between
the federal and state governments to discern what kinds of support
are more appropriate to one level than to another and how support
from these two sources ought to be related. They do need to mesh
well with one another so that federal support, by calling for some
sort of matching effort, does not encourage the states to do less. One
illustration of a complementary relationship would be to make it
possible for state scholarship money to follow a student across state
lines. State boundaries are increasingly arbitrary to the student in his
pursuit of higher education.

    The next form of aid deemed unacceptable is income tax
credit for student expenditures. Sixteen percent of the institutions
in the study expressed displeasure over this kind of aid. It has, however, as already noted, a body of strong supporters who find it not
only acceptable but preferred, in contrast to aid via the states which
has many that find it acceptable but relatively few that find it preferable.

    Agreement among sizes and types of institutions appears remarkably high with a few exceptions which are not unexpected. Bachelor's institutions would put categorical grants in ninth place, not seventh, and some very small institutions find it outright unacceptable. Doctor's institutions, however, which get a lot of this aid, would put it only one vote out of first place on the combined preferred and acceptable register.

Educational Responses

In answering the question, "What happens when more goes out than comes in?" we have referred to surpluses and deficits, to unappropriated surplus, other reserves, and funds functioning as endowment. Since private higher education is frequently dealt with in terms that suggest something faintly venal and unscrupulous about the high and ever-rising tuition such institutions charge, it may be that some casual readers of this report will raise their eyebrows at the very notion of surpluses in a supposedly non-profit institution. They may see no harm in trimming down an institution's unappropriated surplus, believing intuitively that a non-profit institution should run a breakeven annual budget. A word of explanation may be in order.

There are no stockholders of accredited private institutions of higher learning, gathering annually in person or by proxy, to decide how to distribute the profits of their enterprise. If the economy is beneficent, the administration efficient, and the public supportive, there often are surplus funds at the end of the year.

A surplus at the end of a year's operation is an important source of growth capital, which a college or university cannot count on getting, except by a special act of external benevolence, from other sources. It means that the institution can do the innovative and imaginative things the public has come to expect of it and which it does well. It can launch a new venture or strengthen one already begun. It can increase the amount of aid it can offer students in need. It can avoid an increase in tuition or, to meet constantly rising costs, make that increase a modest one.

All of these things a college cannot do if it runs a deficit or merely breaks even. An institution barely afloat, with water nearly over the gunwales, has lost much of its maneuverability, its adventurousness, and freedom of experimentation. Its innovation and risk-taking is confined to putting to sea each academic year. Most ominously, it has no protection against storms. A little student unrest, a little decline in enrollment, a little disenchantment among donors, and the ship may founder. The first thing it does in troubled financial seas is jettison cargo.

The cargo an academic institution carries is education. To get an idea what the educational costs of this depressed financial condition are in private institutions—what cargo has been jettisoned —we invited responses to a series of questions. We first asked what effect the changed economic condition has had on the composition of the student body, or conversely, the effect of a changed student body on the financial condition of the institution.

Sixty-five percent of the respondents pointed out that they now have more students requiring financial aid, and requiring more of it. For many institutions this appears to be a direct consequence of an attempt to be more active in the education of the disadvantaged. Not only do these students require aid themselves, but, in contrast to a college's usual expectations of students, these are bringing less or none of the tuition income upon which most private institutions so heavily rely. This makes it impossible for some institutions to raise through student fees what is required for the improvement of program, or even for the maintenance of the present quality. Moreover, disadvantaged students frequently place demands on the college for additional counseling, remedial programs, and the like, thereby raising the cost of the academic program. An institution relying substantially on tuition revenue to pay for those costs must therefore raise its tuition. This puts a squeeze on its middle income students who now must have aid or leave. Increasingly, they are leaving. Institution after institution reported that "the quality of the student body, as judged by traditional means, has declined." The effect of this, in turn, as perceived in some institutions, has been to discourage the faculty, make private fund raising more difficult, and further deter the recruitment of academically good students. Other institutions have not suffered the same decline in academic quality but have lost the freedom to influence the kind of balance and geographical distribution of the student body thought to be commensurate with the goals and objectives of the institution. Most frequently cited in this regard was the lessening of control over the relative proportions of women and men accepted for admission.

A third group of institutions continues to enroll students from the same economic bracket as formerly but, because private college costs have risen more sharply than increases in per capita income, their students now have a more urgent need for help. "For all practical purposes," reports one institution as a voice for many, "we have priced ourselves out of our market."

For all three of these groups the facts are that there are not enough students with both the academic ability and the financial resources—as well as the willingness to commit those resources—to sustain both the quality of the academic program and to provide the economic mix presently obtaining in their institutions. First the student from the low income family, then the student from the middle income family, and finally, in some institutions, even the student from the higher income family may seek financial assistance either out of a desire to be independent of family support, or, in flat rebellion against the rising costs of private higher education, demand some relief from the costs levied against him. Private institutions may encounter even more resistance from this kind of student as it becomes increasingly possible for such students to establish their independence at more attractive cost by establishing residence and paying in-state tuition while attending a tax supported institution in a state different from the one in which their parents reside.

Sixteen percent of the institutions, in responding to the question about the interrelationships between financial exigency and the composition of the student body, indicated that the institution now enrolled more wealthier students than before, while slightly more than 19 percent reported more financially poorer students than formerly. Twelve percent reported that they were restricted in the extent of their recruiting among lower income groups by their financial limitations. Because of the economic polarization reported on some campuses and because of the open-ended nature of the question, the same institution could report both more wealthier and more poorer students. Nine percent of the respondents specifically cited fewer middle income students, although this is clearly also true when an institution reports a larger percentage of wealthier and poorer students.

Six percent indicated that the college had more women students as a consequence of its financial situation while 41 institutions, largely colleges for women, reported that they had gone or were going coed as a result of the same financial condition.

Nearly one-third reported a relationship between the economic condition and enrollment growth. It was a mixed bag. Some resorted to growth as a way out of a deficit condition or as a way to avoid one, while others found themselves in their present condition as a result of enrollment growth. Apparently, as Jenny and Wynn have found,[2] enrollment growth at the right rate can be an effective device for keeping costs per student down, but it must be at the right rate and it must be sustained. If it is neither, then, as some of these institutions have found, it adds to rather than subtracts from the problem.

Only 13 percent of the institutions reported no change in the composition of the student body in relation to the college's economic condition and only 3 percent had no response.

The frequencies of these several responses were roughly similar both geographically and by enrollment and degree level groups. One striking exception is the much higher percentage of academically poorer students reported among the Small institutions and among the Doctor's institutions. For all private institutions, about two and one-half times as many institutions report an influx of academically less competent students as report more academically competent students. For the Small enrollment group it is five times and for the Doctor's degree group it is seven times.

We also asked our responding institutions to tell us what programs—programs they had reasonable aspirations of achieving—had been foregone as a result of their financial stress. It is apparent from their answers to this question that private colleges and universities are abreast of what their needs are and of developments in higher education, and that they are not—if the words reasonable aspirations are as meaningful as I think they are—neglecting their

[2] Jenny and Wynn, *The Golden Years,* p. 57.

planning for program development because of their financial depression. It is also apparent, however, that grave shortages exist in private higher education because of the financial stress in which they find themselves.

The answers fell into four categories: programs and courses not begun; faculty development put off; capital equipment not purchased; and construction delayed. Often these are intertwined. Programs cannot develop because faculty and equipment cannot be brought up to standard; and top-flight faculty members have been difficult to attract where equipment has been poor and facilities lacking.

Over 50 percent of our respondents were able to point to specific programs and courses for which plans had been completed and implementation had been intended, often with first steps already taken, but which have been placed in a holding category. These are often programs at the advancing edge of academe for which there is much demand: black studies, urban studies, environmental programs, honors programs, non-western studies programs. Faculty development is another aspiration put off by financial necessity. This includes increasing the number of faculty, improving their quality, raising their salaries, improving their fringe benefits, and inaugurating sabbatical programs. Equipment is another area where an expected and needed advance has not been forthcoming. A full quarter of the institutions lament their inability to expand their library holdings. A third of the responses point to unfilled needs for science and laboratory equipment, computers and other capital equipment, and other general educational and teaching equipment.

And then there are buildings which have not been built or renovated, facilities which the institution judges it needs if it is to stay in the running as an academically competitive institution of higher learning. The facility most frequently mentioned (by a quarter of the institutions) as needing renovation, extension, or rebuilding, is the library. Next most frequently mentioned (by one-fifth of the institutions) is a building for the performing and fine arts. Academic buildings (classrooms, language laboratories) were also listed by one-fifth of the institutions. Physical education facilities are needed by 17 percent of the institutions, science buildings by 14 percent, and student centers, health centers, and other buildings.

As Alan Pifer perceptively noted, an institution does not move from vigorous life to death.[3] Its demise "is more likely to be a protracted and inconspicious process lasting many years and encompassing several stages of progressive debility." The first stage, and the one at which it should be considered seriously ill, is when it can no longer make vigorous response to new challenges. That is the significance of these programs foregone because of financial restrictions. They represent the first stage in an inconspicuous process of progressive debility. "With more money," as one respondent observed, "we can do a significantly better job, and a bigger one as well." Without it, "we may not be able to survive."

We asked our respondents one final question in this series. It was a harsh one and we almost decided—after virtually unanimous negative response from the institutions which pilot-tested the questionnaire—to eliminate it. After asking what programs had not been initiated due to financial restrictions, we asked, "Have any programs slipped academically for the same reason?"

To our surprise a large number of institutions responded. Not many (5 percent) acknowledged in stark language that the quality of faculty or of academic program had actually slipped. However, over one fifth of the institutions responded somewhat obliquely by pointing to programs that had been cut out altogether. Foreign languages, drama, art, were the most frequent victims, but a wide range of programs felt the axe somewhere.

One-quarter (with some overlap from the previous group) pointed to programs already in existence that had not advanced. These were apt to be bread-and-butter courses dwarfed at some primitive stage of development by a shortage of funds: one or one-and-one-half man departments that do not expand; development of undergraduate and graduate programs in basic sciences that are set back indefinitely; special programs for underprivileged and minority students that must be held to an ineffectual level of operation. Another 10 percent asserted that no slippage had taken place, yet. But they were fearful.

It took courage to respond to this question at all, and institu-

[3] Alan Pifer, "The Jeopardy of Private Institutions," in *Annual Report: Carnegie Corporation of New York* (New York, 1970), p. 9.

tions are not to be faulted for replying to it in circumlocutory fashion. What kinds of cuts in the academic program and how many such cuts constitute a serious limitation on an institution's program may be subject to wide ranges of interpretation. To take an extreme example, but a factual one, one college reported that although it was unable to fill necessary appointments in a critical science area it had not slipped. It was simply not offering any courses in that area for the time being.

One final word. Some good things are happening as a result of this financial stringency. One of the most important—reported by over 50 percent of the institutions—is that faculty members have begun to accept the reality of this financial crisis at their own institutions. They have begun to respond to that awareness by reexamining their demands on the budget, by looking more positively on inter-institutional cooperation as a way to cut costs, by establishing priorities among possible expenditure items, by refining institutional objectives and reviewing requests for new courses in the light of those objectives, and even by assisting in attracting students to the institution. Trustees have assumed a greater role in the area of fund raising; and management information systems and planning, programming, and budgeting systems have been given a boost as have long-range planning, tighter control on expenditures, and better budgeting in general.

A greater attention to cost accounting (reported by 42 percent of the colleges and universities) is especially encouraging as is the finer definition of goals and objectives (What is the institution really here for?) reported by 38 percent of the institutions. Forty-five percent say that their financial difficulties have prompted the development of better fund-raising techniques.

Five percent of our respondents thought that we were mad to inquire after benefits. One wondered if our computer would recognize sarcasm (it did) and another granted that there were benefits to impending insolvency but the wear and tear on everybody's nervous system make them of less value than a list of them might suggest.

Many of these benefits are not spurious, however, and, what is more, hold promise of being lasting. If greater support from the outside is forthcoming and the competitive situation with tax-supported institutions is eased, most of these institutions can have a viable future. The question is, will those external adjustments be large enough and soon enough?

Basic Steps to Regain Solvency

A challenge to grow is one of the suggestions certain to be presented to an institution with greater outlays than income. This suggestion is natural within a society that follows a banner exalting growth (Excelsior!) as the impetus that moves the entire society—not merely our economy or higher education—forward. As an answer to the specific problem in higher education, moreover, growth promises fuller utilization of plant. Growth would make possible an increase in the student faculty ratio. Growth might permit the employment of additional faculty at junior levels as well as the enlargement and enrichment of program. Growth would fill up the residence hall spaces and add to tuition income. Growth creates an atmosphere of dynamism and buoys morale. Besides, the ten-year plan for the institution calls for growth.

Prescribing growth as a remedy for the ills of the private institution today is similar to prescribing youth as a cure for the debilities of old age. Both would have beneficent effects; but disillusionment is the likely condition of those who believe that any physician can deliver the remedy in substantial amounts. Growth in the private sector (specific institutions to the contrary notwithstanding) is very unlikely. Even in the public sector, only moderate growth is likely through 1978 (and that not true of all types of public institutions). After 1978, a yearly decline for at least seven years is currently forecast by the National Education Association.

Some single-sex colleges are under the impression that becoming coeducational will double their student market. While this change will very likely make them more attractive to the sex already attending the institution, and may, if it is a prestigious college for men, increase its total student market substantially, it is a delusion to believe that the market doubles simply because there are approximately as many men as women. As Humphrey Doermann notes, the number of students with both the academic ability and the money needed to attend most private institutions is substantially less than the total pool of prospective college students of college age. Those that do possess the qualifications are already well cultivated by other institutions and do not constitute a new market.[4]

If growth from the traditional college age group is unrealistic for the private sector as a whole, where should it put its hope? The answer is easier in the negative than in the affirmative: Its hope does not lie in the number of gold stars it is awarded for correctly responding to a list of suggestions regarding minute or irrelevant expenditure items. Even if an institution has turned off the heat in the hockey area, as one such checklist seriously advised, salvation will probably elude it. A slate unsullied by venial sins of management will not save the institution that commits the mortal ones. This is not to argue that the management of institutions of higher learning cannot be improved. It can be; and the better managed institutions are the quickest to acknowledge this and to work to achieve still better management. Wiser future planning and budgeting, both short and long range, are especially and urgently needed in far more institutions. Before an institution becomes totally preoccupied with the finer points of management, however, it must attend to its first priority.

What an institution needs first is an attractive academic program. The private institutions in this study include undegraduate liberal arts colleges. These institutions remember the days when the education they offered was the normative description of all education pursued beyond high school. Going on to college meant attending a four-year liberal arts institution. Then, in accommodation to the community colleges, the term college was superseded by the term higher education. This, in turn, under the growing weight of the education and vocational training offered under proprietary and corporation auspices, and the need to plan systems of education accordingly, is giving way to the still larger term post-secondary education.

Colleges which are no longer the automatic route to be followed by every student continuing education beyond the high school have two basic options; both of them valid. One is to redefine

[4] Humphrey Doermann, "The Student Market for Private Colleges," *Liberal Education*, 1970, 56(2), 295.

a liberal education in a way that is more responsive to the contemporary student's quest for relevance and meaning. There is no one proper formula for doing this. Each institution must shape an academic program that is appropriate to its own constituents and that is informed by its own value commitments. This last is especially important for it is frequently the absence of a perceived value-based orientation that gives the liberal arts their hollow sound. If contemporary students are to be attracted to the excitement of liberal education, the institutions that offer it must be articulate in giving expression to these commitments.

For some institutions this reformulation of liberal education should be dramatic. It should include: a reorganization of knowledge seeking to offer unity rather than fragmented specialization; an approach to learning in which cognitive methods may be supplemented by other modes of knowing; a redefinition of an educated man which goes beyond his ability to technically manipulate the data elements of knowledge; a fresh approach to the purposes of education which may include a reshaping of the physical and cultural world.

The other route (which need not necessarily be sharply separated from the first) is to reshape the institution along more frankly career lines and thereby develop alternative student markets. Few of these institutions have been altogether detached from the vocational aspirations of their students in the past. (For instance, a very healthy percentage of their students graduated with the credentials necessary to begin teaching at elementary and secondary levels of education.) If the vocational interests of today's students have changed, these institutions may change also. The growth of work-study programs and the development of career (and second career) programs for persons older than the college age generation are evidence that many already have. But some ought to consider going further still, including possible links with the proprietary sector, or at least with programs normally offered only under such auspices.

The institution's top priority is its academic program; but there are also management improvements that could make significant changes in the economic health of the institution. One of these is a set of suggestions put forward by Howard Bowen and Gordon Douglass which involves the use of a wide range of instructional methods that would raise the productivity level of the institution.[5] It is, unhappily, easier to introduce these changes into an expanding institution than into a contracting one. The very institutions in greatest need of effecting these changes and enjoying the consequent economic benefits, therefore, are the same institutions that will find it most difficult to make the changes. These changes, however, could be effected over a period of time. An institution can begin to implement these suggestions when certain situations, such as faculty retirements, present the opportunity for implementation. If, as the Committee for Economic Development's 1973 report on *The Management and Financing of Colleges* glumly forecasts, future government support on a per student basis will remain constant in real terms, then proposals for increased learning productivity cannot be casually disregarded.

Very small colleges face special problems, partly because smallness does not appear to be especially prized today as an American virtue. The benefits of smallness are frequently extolled, for other people. When the chips are down, we make our purchases from large companies, not small ones; we shop at giant supermarkets, not corner grocery stores; we live in large urban areas, not small towns; and, typically, we attend large institutions, not very small colleges. We do these things partly out of necessity but also because we prefer bigness. Some of us may miss the intimacy and service of the corner grocery, but most of us prefer the variety, the speed, and the anonymity of the large supermarket. In the fall of 1937, according to Donald J. Reichard, institutions enrolling under 500 students constituted 44 percent of the colleges and universities in the United States and enrolled 18 percent of the students attending institutions of higher learning. Thirty years later they constituted 27 percent of the institutions and accounted for 2 percent of the students. That decline is apt to continue.

Most very small institutions are not rich enough to be as small as they are. All institutions are vulnerable at the point of declining enrollments, but the very small institution is especially

[5] Howard R. Bowen and Gordon K. Douglass, *Efficiency in Liberal Education: A Study of Comparative Instructional Costs for Different Ways of Organizing Teaching-Learning in a Liberal Arts College* (New York, 1971).

vulnerable because each student loss means that the fixed costs must be absorbed by a smaller student body or be offset by endowment or other income. Since it is also a characteristic of very small colleges that they tend to have small endowments, a drop in enrollment means that the cost per remaining student rises more precipitously than in larger institutions and must either be reflected in increased tuition or in institutional deficits. Since tuitions are already high, the result is apt to be an institutional deficit rather than increased tuition, although it may be both. Very small colleges need larger per student financial buffers than larger institutions. Typically, very small colleges do not have these additional resources. As they find it increasingly difficult to compete with other institutions, therefore, many of them ought to pursue merger possibilities. Only a merger or a strong federation will be able to effect the kinds of changes that might permit efficient operation.

This report ends *in medias res,* as it were. The final destiny of private higher education is presaged in the foregoing pages, but the future still holds promise for most of these institutions if the will to preserve them exists in the public sector, among their friends, and within the institutions themselves.

Representative
Nature of Study

❉❀❉❀❉❀❉❀❉❀❉❀❉❀❉❀❉❀❉❀❉❀

This study was undertaken to assemble up-to-date hard financial data on all accredited private higher education, and to analyze and evaluate these in order to present a solidly based description of the current situation. Very little can be safely said about all of higher education on the strength of an analysis of a few institutions if it is not firmly bolted both to reliable hard data and to a statistically secure sample. What we sought, therefore, was to survey, through hard data, the financial status of *all* private, four-year, accredited institutions of higher learning. We did this through a questionnaire sent to all but twenty-nine of such colleges and universities in the nation.

The response to the questionnaire, especially in view of its thoroughness and complexity, was, astonishingly, in excess of 75 percent, a very healthy basis for making statements about all of private higher education. This is a tribute to the questionnaire itself, which looked as though it was asking the right questions; to the confidence of member institutions in the Association of American Colleges, which sponsored the study; and to the acuteness of the private sector's concern for its financial problems.

Even so, one may wonder how the non-respondents (including the handful not invited to participate in the study in the first place) compare with the ones that responded with completed copies of the questionnaire.

Starting with the twenty-nine institutions that were not sent the questionnaire, they are, so far as we can judge, the only private colleges and universities that met the criteria for the study but were not members of the Association of American Colleges. Since we were about to ask colleges and universities to invest a substantial amount of time in providing data normally regarded as highly confidential, and since we were unable to determine on the face of things that the non-member institutions were different in any material way from member institutions, we did not send the questionnaire to non-members. We reasoned that while we had some claim to the attention of our own members we could not make the same prima facie case for the attention of non-members.

If we add together the non-members (29) and the members that were invited to participate but failed to return a complete questionnaire in time to be included in the study (179) and make some comparisons with responding institutions (554) in several ways readily available to us, the following results emerge.

Adding responding and non-responding institutions together in order to arrive at a distribution of all accredited four-year private colleges and universities by various demographic characteristics, and then comparing the percentage our responding institutions make on the same analysis, we find a virtual match in every instance, as the following data indicate.

On geographical distribution, for example, the furthest deviation is found in the West North Central region. As a whole, this region contains 12 percent of all private colleges and universities, but 15 percent of our responding institutions. The group of institutions included in this study, therefore, tends to be slightly over-representative of institutions in the upper west midwest. No other region deviates by more than 1 percent.

The Pacific Region (8 percent of the institutions in the study) includes California, Oregon, Washington, Hawaii, and Alaska. Mountain (2 percent) includes Arizona, Colorado, Idaho, Montana, Nevada, New Mexico, Utah, and Wyoming. West South Central (5 percent) includes Arkansas, Louisana, Oklahoma, and Texas. East South Central (7 percent) includes Alabama, Kentucky, Mississippi, and Tennessee. West North Central (15 percent) includes Iowa, Kansas, Minnesota, Missouri, Nebraska, North Dakota, and South Dakota. East North Central (20 percent) includes Illinois, Indiana, Michigan, Ohio, and Wisconsin. South Atlantic (14 percent) includes Delaware, Florida, Georgia, Maryland, North Carolina, South Carolina, Virginia, West Virginia, and the District of Columbia. Mid-Atlantic (20 percent) includes New York, New Jersey, and Pennsylvania. New England (9 percent) includes Connecticut, Maine, Massachusetts, New Hampshire, Rhode Island, and Vermont.

Our comparisons on the basis of enrollment ranges and degree levels bear out the same picture, namely, that our responding institutions are highly representative of all private institutions in the country.

The population of institutions included in our study is classified by five enrollment range levels: Smallest (500 and below, 6 percent of the institutions), Small (501–1000, 34 percent), Medium (1001–2000, 37 percent), Large (2001–4000, 12 percent), and Largest (4001 up, 11 percent). The percentage figures for the national totals and for the responding institutions in our study are equal for two of the five categories and 1 or 2 percent apart for each of the other categories. Our respondents tend to be a hair light in representing institutions enrolling 500 or less and a shade heavy in representing institutions enrolling between one and two thousand students.

Of all private four-year and above accredited colleges and universities, those whose highest offering is a four or five year baccalaureate degree comprise 61 percent of the total and 61 percent of our responding colleges. Those offering a master's degree but not higher comprise 27 percent of the total and 28 percent of ours. Those offering the doctorate are 12 percent of the whole and 11 percent of ours. Our analyses typically include five degree levels:

Bachelor's (four or five year baccalaureate degree), Limited Master's (master's degree in no more than three areas), Master's (master's degree in four areas or more), Limited Doctor's (doctor's degree in no more than three areas), Doctor's (doctor's degree in four or more areas).

There is an obvious temptation for the casual reader to lay one analysis on top of another—enrollment level on top of degree level, for example—on the assumption that size and degree level are virtually coterminous. This is true only in a very broad sense.

While it is true that no Ph.D. granting institution enrolls fewer than 500 students, for instance, it is not true that those enrolling more than 4000 students are all Ph.D. granting institutions. Indeed, 34 percent are not, and two such institutions offer nothing higher than the baccalaureate. Very little can safely be assumed about the degree level of institutions enrolling between two and four thousand students or about the enrollment level of institutions offering the master's degree in four or more areas.

It may be worth noting, while we are comparing these various grids, that 34 of the 59 institutions in our study which offer the doctorate are independent of church relationship; sixteen are Roman Catholic related, four are Methodist, and there are five others. Twelve major denominational groups reporting in this study have no colleges offering work beyond the masters and several smaller ones offer nothing beyond the baccalaureate. Thus, although independent institutions form slightly less than 30 percent of the total number of institutions in our study, they constitute 58 percent of the doctoral granting institutions.

We were also able to make an analysis on the basis of denominational affiliation or lack thereof. Here again the ratio each group bears to the total of our responding institutions is nearly identical to its proportion to the total of all private institutions in the nation. Roman Catholic institutions, for example, comprise 28 percent of all private colleges and universities in the nation and 29 percent of the institutions responding to our study. Methodist-related institutions are 11 percent of the national total and 11 percent of our responding institutions. Our study slightly underrepresents the independent colleges and universities. They comprise 31 percent of the national total and make up a slightly smaller 29 percent of our responding group.

On the basis of these demographic comparisons, the institutions in our study appear representative of all private institutions of higher learning. We believe, therefore, that the data on our institutions provide a reasonably stable basis for reliable estimates of comparable values for the total population.

Index